How God does Happiness

A thought for every day of the year

Tim Daniel

Acknowledgements

To Kasey and Abbey, who somehow knew not to accept anything until it was genuinely interesting and helpful.

Prologue

A highway sign in a parched desert that reads "Ocean beaches, 90 miles ahead" is not the ocean. Those words can't begin to convey the vastness, power, and mysteries of the ocean. It would be absurd to stop, get out our beach chairs, and sit next to the sign.

The words in this book are intended to function as directional signs only. They cannot contain or limit God. The best they can do is to point in the general direction of God and away from the many enticing but dangerous mirages that appear in the vast wasteland along the way.

Entire worlds of mirage have come and gone, leaving wasted lives and shattered empires in their wake.

There are things that appear to be sacred but are not, as they involve cruelties God would never be part of.

Once we learn to spot the difference between a true and false signal, we happily heed a "don't go there" signal from God. There is no need to repeat deadly mistakes from the past even if they appear in a new enticing form.

Day 1

It takes about 365 days for the earth to orbit all the way around the sun one time. A year is not limited to January 1 to December 31. A new year starts every day on any day.

This day is the start of a new journey. We will cover new ground and explore unfamiliar places where a new kind of happiness can be found, God's happiness.

God does happiness but goes about it differently. What unfolds in us is new. What happens around us is better.

God's happiness makes all the difference in the world in how much we enjoy life, because it changes how we enjoy life and how much life we enjoy.

God's happiness is the only thing that can make our world different.

We don't come to God looking for the world's happiness. If we do, we find nothing but a hurtful silence which makes us angry at God.

Day 2

There are two kinds of happiness just like there are two ways of keeping time.

One uses clocks and calendars and is essential to fit us into a vast production-consumption machine.

With the other, older way our mind uses signals from the environment to tell us when to get up and when to go to sleep.

We notice how the plants and animals around us behave to know what season it is and when it is time to prepare for winter.

This kind of timekeeping is essential to fit us into Life on Earth.

So is God's happiness.

Day 3

God's happiness is not something we chase, hoard and try to hold onto.

God's happiness is something that catches up to us later and surprises us.

It is worth waiting for because it is so satisfying.

God's happiness lasts and grows into something we can't hold and hoard.
It is just too big. It spills out into our world causing more of itself.

God's happiness survives unpleasant circumstances because it is not built out of pleasant circumstances in the first place.

Day 4

God's happiness makes use of sadness just as a ship makes use of water, by floating *in* it, not escaping *from* it.

God's happiness does not flee sadness. Nor does it banish pain.

The deeper the sadness, the heavier the load, the greater the pain, the stronger happiness must be to make productive use of it.

Only God's happiness is that strong.

Day 5

God's happiness is something we *learn* to enjoy.

Like living without clocks and calendars at first it seems strange.

We welcome its strangeness for some time until one day we realize we prefer it and would miss it if it went away.

At first it's like learning a foreign language.

The best way to learn a new language is by living where it is spoken, immersing yourself in it, learning all its odd quirks and surprising eloquence.

Once it all starts to make sense you wouldn't want it to be any different.

Day 6

Where do we go to immerse ourselves in God's happiness as a language?

In nature.

Go where you can observe nature doing what it wants the way it wants to do it.

It can be as small as a windowsill or as large as a forest.

Go there often enough and stay long enough, silent enough until, using all your senses, you start to sense something you didn't know was there, but that you enjoy.
 Somehow it just feels *right*.

Try to put a name to that something.
Your name for it is as good as anyone else's.

Day 7

We are surprised by God's happiness as we see how our needs are met.

To get anything done how much do you need?
Enough.

When do you need it?
When you will be using it.

Where do you need it?
Where it will be used.

How long do you need it?
Until you don't anymore.

Just enough, just in time, at the place you need it for as long as you need it - to do well what God created you to do.

Day 8

There is no waste in God's happiness.

If something isn't supplied we don't need it yet. If it is needed it is supplied.

Hording is wasteful.
We hoard to prevent worry.

Once we experience how God does happiness we stop worrying so much.

Worry ruins happiness.
Wonder sustains it.

God's happiness brings us into a contagious state of rapt attention, amazement, and gratitude.

Day 9

The way God supplies happiness is to pack a lot of joy into a little package.

We become quiet, pay attention, and slowly absorb something wonderful that costs no money.

We get more out of an ounce of what God put in our path for free, than it is possible to get out of a ton of what you must pay a lot of money for.

God's happiness is high in absorption and low in consumption.

We are surprised we can feel so happy with so little for so long, so consistently.

Day 10

Surprise is a big part of God's happiness.

Disappointment is a bad surprise.
Delight is a good surprise.

God does not disappoint.

We delight more and more in God's direction as we see more of the same kind of order and fruitfulness unfold in our own lives as we see in nature.

Somehow It feels new and fresh, and at the same time ancient and familiar.

It is a kind of homecoming.
We sense we are where we belong.

Day 11

God's happiness is indirect.

It is a by-product of things we do for reasons stronger than our need for personal happiness.

Day 12

Personal happiness draws from the stock of happiness created by a community of lives.

God's goal is a shared happiness larger than my own personal bliss. The Creator intends all creatures to be happy, not just me, and not just the groups I belong to.

God only draws near to those who want most what their Creator also wants most.

Shared goals and shared labor are what make true friendship.

The happiness of God is knowing friendship with God.

Day 13

When God is near things get interesting.

The daily freshness of God's moral direction keeps us from living in boredom or smug certainty.

We have boring hours, but we are not tedious people living boring lives.

We learn God will meet us in what we are to do, but we are never certain ahead of time just how and when we will be met.

The way God meets us is never the same, but it always acts to increase our capacity to add to the stock of happiness other lives can count on.

Day 14

I cry out to God in my pain, in silence, in solitude, near something else God created.

I wait. I listen.
The Creator draws near.

I am met.
I am taught a new way.

I am aided when something unexpected happens that makes new behavior possible.

Later I am so happy I went through that. My fear of life begins to heal.

Life starts to make sense.
My trust in life begins to grow.
I feel better equipped to face whatever comes next.

Day 15

God's happiness keeps us young.

We are curious and fascinated. We learn, explore, try things, practice, fail, improve, and try again. We leave old situations and dead institutions.

We unlearn old habits.
We stretch ourselves.

After struggling with a problem, we finally work our way through it until there is a moment of triumph, when a newly acquired ability overcomes a discouraging limitation we have lived with for years.

We feel fully alive inside.
It is thrilling and deeply meaningful.

Day 16

God's Happiness is daily.
It catches up with us in 24-hour increments.

We can't do anything about yesterday, except accept
responsibility for any harm we may have caused and
start to clean up the mess.

We can realize the day is a gift and watch for ways to do
the most good with it that we can, because God does
not promise any creature a tomorrow.

What God gives us is today.
This day could be our last one on earth, or the last one
we share with someone we love.

Day 17

How will I behave today?

Whose purposes will I pursue?

Those who live each day in service of God's purposes *for* earth start to see God's happiness grow *on* earth, in the relationships around them.

They find that as they harm less and help more they too are harmed less and helped more, but in new ways that could not have been anticipated or controlled.

For those serving the Creator's interests on earth life becomes safer, less lonely, and more intriguing.

Day 18

God's happiness is careful.

What will we do with our time and attention?

Will we cause more happiness on earth, or more misery?

The more God's happiness shows up in and around our lives, the more we become an oasis of caring in a desert of callousness.

An oasis does not need to advertise.

Word gets out.

Day 19

God's happiness often lies on the other side of something we initially wanted to avoid.

Sometimes what we must do to make earth happier for one of God's creatures is inconvenient, but it is the right thing to do.

Right now, all we can see is the cost of doing it.

We grumble inside but do it anyway.

Because it has happened repeatedly, we learn to sense that something good lies on the other side of this choice.

It will show up later and satisfy our souls in ways we can't imagine now.

Day 20

When God places one of us in any situation, it is not long before things stop getting worse and start getting better.

People treat each other more carefully.

They take better care of any other creature that depends on them to survive and thrive.

And they do thrive.
Together.

This makes God very happy.

When God's happiness overflows it carries in its flow to a state of deep, peaceful awe. We feel humbled because we know we didn't give this happiness to ourselves.

Day 21

We abandon God's happiness when we run away...

From caring for another life.

From facing a difficult situation and finding a solution.

Day 22

God's happiness catches up and meets us....

While caring for another life
In a difficult situation that demands a just response.

Day 23

God's happiness beams in the amazing fit between the type of problem and type of the solution we actively participate in finding.

A qualitative problem can only be satisfied by a qualitative solution.

A bigger house will not make loneliness hurt less. Only a good relationship can do that.

A good relationship can thrive in a small house.

Day 24

More is often a cheap substitute for *better*. God does not do cheap substitutes.

God only does the real thing.

To chase cheap substitutes, we must leave the warmth of God's happiness.

The absence of God's happiness is a cold, lifeless void.

Day 25

God's happiness is resilient. It can take a blow and recover.

It can enter a new, unfamiliar situation and adjust quickly until it again produces a wider happiness, one that includes more than just us.

A resilient happiness is one that works *because of* the forces it draws upon, and *despite* the forces fighting against it.

God's resilient happiness gets us through tough times, and we come out the other side better equipped to face what comes next.

Day 26

The mark of fragile happiness is cowardice. Fragile happiness will not risk itself for the well-being of someone else or to defend a noble idea.

Cowards are miserable people.
The mark of resilient happiness is courage.
We discover that if we stay *on* God's side in the contest, and *by* God's side to receive direction, we are never alone.

We are always met.
We are always helped.

This gives us the confidence to risk our own well-being when necessary to protect the well-being of others.

Active, sustained courage is the only way to make sure noble ideas are not just empty slogans.

History teaches us that courage in service of a noble idea is contagious, gathering up and focusing the force of many people into something to strike terror in the heart of a predator.

Day 27

God gave us our conscience to help keep us *on* God's side and *by* God's side. When we are about to cross an ethical line our conscience bothers us. Once across the line our conscience disturbs our sleep.

Our conscience is the law of God written in our DNA as a social species. This law will speak to us when we have quieted ourselves enough to hear it. It warns us we are about to do something that will weaken the very force of collective kindness we ourselves will need someday.

We feel the fear that danger lies around this blind corner - because it does. God gave us that fear for a reason. It is where profound learning starts.

Under the power of conscience, we stop.
We cry out to God.
We ask for wisdom.
We must find another way besides crossing that line.

We fall silent and listen.
We know we don't know what is best to do in this situation, but we know God does.

Day 28

God's way to happiness will always be simpler than what we were doing before, and simpler than what we once thought we had to do to be happy.

God's way will involve subtracting steps more than adding them.

There will be fewer things that *can* go wrong, so fewer things *do* go wrong. We find we can afford to worry less.

There will be fewer things to defend so there will be fewer fights. We find we can afford to drop some of our defenses.

The energy we get back is refreshing.

Day 29

God's simple happiness hums right along when the power goes out and the last battery dies.

God's happiness sustained people a thousand years ago and sustains people now with no access to the latest technology.

God's happiness does not require a large audience or a carefully staged performance.

Rather, God's happiness peaks in the silence of solitude, away from all technology.

Day 30

Why does God's happiness peak in solitude?

Because all bad things start there, in bitter internal conversations.

Good things start when we quiet ourselves enough, long enough, to hear the quiet voice of the One utterly beyond ourselves...

Who exists independently of us...

Who is better than us...

Who knows better than us...

One whose concern includes our concerns but doesn't begin and end with them, as if we were the center of the universe.

Day 31

God makes us helpful to life by first removing from us what is harmful to life.

Solitude is the place where we ask God to remove those harmful things.

Solitude is God's repair shop.

Why not in a group?

Because destructive behaviors must stop where they start – in the privacy of our own hearts. We can deceive ourselves. We can deceive others. We can't deceive God.

God knows our deepest dishonesties and how to shine a painful light on them. It is the only way lasting change can happen in our lives and in our world.

Day 32

God re-constructs our souls from the inside out.

It does not happen fast.
It is not a once-for-all event.

Under God's gentle touch our souls discharge useless material daily. Our bodies also discharge waste daily. It is only natural, and just as necessary for our health and happiness.

Day 33

The repair work eventually replaces what we do that bothers our conscience.

It also confronts why we keep doing it despite all our efforts to behave differently. There are a few critical things we can't fix ourselves.

When we fix those things ourselves, they break again.

Another, objective, wiser mind, with a more precise hand, must take charge.

Day 34

God creates unforeseen events and uses them to alter the way we put ourselves together on the inside.

When God repairs a long-standing defect it stays repaired, if we continue our daily meetings.

Between two who have a good history together 10 minutes can be enough to make real progress on something.

We have longer, more open-ended sessions with God on days when we have more rested time available. But we never go a day without opening our souls to God's presence and ethical guidance with the full intent to follow the guidance we receive.

Day 35

To know God is to love God.

There is nothing we enjoy more than spending time alone with the one we love.

We relish that time. It is the first thing we desire and the last thing we want to skip.

We build it into our lives first, then put in everything else.

We protect that time.

Day 36

God's gentle presence grows outward from our solitude to our attitudes, to our habits, to our primary relationships, to our work, to our citizenship.

God's presence shows up in how we treat neighbors and strangers.

God's presence shows up in how we treat animals and children; those who have less power than us.

Day 37

As God's presence grows it governs more of our lives, especially our unplanned reactions to unforeseen events.

In those moments God's ruling presence shows in our spontaneous facial expressions and words. In our unstaged reactions, those who interact with us regularly see who we really are. They see our first reaction, then our second reaction.

The average of the two reveals who we really are.

Day 38

Humans are free to choose how to live. To choose we need options.

Those in constant contact with us have a realistic alternative to consider after seeing God's happiness rule a life like theirs in unhappy circumstances.

For those closest to us we present a better case study than any famous person can be, because our loved ones aren't famous either.

Day 39

How will I know if God's happiness is ruling more of my life?

I monitor my complaining.
How often do I complain? How bad does it get? Does it include tantrums?
How long does it last?

If I complain often, if it goes on for a long time, if it gets ugly – I don't yet have enough of God's happiness to provide an option for others. They know when I have a setback I behave no differently than them, so why should they bother seeking God?

It's best to hold off communicating with others for now. They already have their own complaints; they won't benefit from hearing about mine.

Day 40

When I complain I am saying...

God got it wrong.
God mismanaged my affairs, so I cannot trust God.
Clearly God does not know best.
I know better.
I know how everything will work out in the future, what will and will not make me happy.

Do I really believe that?

Day 41

When I start to complain less often, when it doesn't last as long, and when it is not as bad as it used to be – God's happiness is starting to displace resentment, just as light dispels darkness.

I recover from setbacks quicker than I used to, turning them into new problem-solving capacities.

I emerge from the setbacks a bit more trusting, more available, and more useful to God.

Day 42

One day it dawns on me; had I not found myself in that difficult situation I initially thought God "mismanaged" I would have had no need to become more capable.

I like the feeling of becoming more resilient and capable.

I don't go looking for them, but I tend to be a bit less hostile to the next unavoidable difficult situation.

I rise to meet the next difficult situation a bit faster. I may not complain aloud at all. I keep it inside.

I am a bit calmer and kinder around others.

Over time those bits add up.
God is changing me from the inside out.

God trusts me to handle more situations the way God handles things without making them worse.

That means God's happiness can extend to places it couldn't have before.

Day 43

Something else tracks my movement toward God's happiness:

Laughter.

I can even laugh at myself!

When I laugh more and whine less it means I am getting into a rhythm with God.

Together we are moving faster to a better place.

I can feel it.

Others can feel it too and will want to join in so as not to miss out.

It is a kind of happy migration.

Day 44

God's happiness is an open secret, hiding in plain sight.

It is not a closed secret, available only to those privileged with beauty, youth, health, money, fame, power, status, or genius.

An example of one of God's open secrets is how healthy soil can grow almost anything.

Find some healthy soil and examine it closely, using your eyes and nose and fingers. It starts to explain itself to you.

The greatest privilege on earth is to be met and taught by God. God's academy is open to anyone who makes the time to pay attention. Attention is the tuition.

Day 45

Solitude in God's presence is rich, fertile soil.

From it a new colony of life can grow.

On rare occasions we must skip our time with God to take care of something that needs urgent attention. But we don't habitually neglect that time, any more than a wise gardener would neglect her soil for months to build a greenhouse.

She makes time for both.

Daily is best, but we always make rested time to be with God over the course of the week.

We are eager to return.
It is the place we feel most at home.

Day 46

We protect our time alone with God because it is the only thing that can reliably equip us to be useful on earth.

There is a sequence to it.

We attend to God's needs.
God attends to our needs.
We then go out and attend to the needs of those God has entrusted into our care.

To attend means to show up, to stretch, and to deal with.

God does not ask us to ignore our own needs. We bring them to God.

God sorts through them.

Our Creator alone knows the difference between what we really need and what we think we need.

Sometimes we are wrong about what we think we need.

When we are wrong, typically we think we are missing out on something praised by the culture around us.

That is where most of our errors start.

God stretches our understanding of what is good and necessary for happiness beyond what our culture taught us to envy.

Day 47

As God gently exposes and corrects our errors, we feel remorse.

It is painful, but pain creates a memory that is stronger than any memory pleasure can create.

This leaves a boundary in our minds we will not want to cross again. We are now much less likely to cross that boundary the next time we approach it.

We are now more tenderhearted than before.

We see the pain of others faster and feel it more deeply.

We become more precise and careful as a result.

We become as gentle with others as God is with us.

We stay as accessible to them as God is to us.

We follow up to see how they are doing.

We follow up on our promises in a timely manner.

They do not feel ignored or neglected.

Leaving our errors in place we would have causes us to do more harm than good in our attempts to help ourselves or others.

The acute pain we feel as God removes an error subsides, the new effectiveness remains.

God leaves enough living remorse that we don't want to repeat the error that caused harm to another creature.

Day 48

We can get so busy doing good that we skip time alone with God.

We think we can afford to skip this time since we already know the best thing to do today and how to do it.

In our certainty and haste, we are mean to those we see as blocking our efforts to do good.

Those we harm most often are those who are only

trying to help.

This is not God's way.

We are not yet ready to be helpful to God.

Day 49

With our errors still in place we hurt most deeply those we love the most.

The result of our uncorrected errors is to increase the stock of unhappiness on earth, even as we work to "change the world."

All we have done is to perpetuate precisely what we intended to change.

Day 50

Think of what is essential for life: clean air, gravity, clean water, sunshine. Remove one of those for any length of time and life withers away.

Is happiness not also essential for life?

If so, then happiness is essential for *every* life, for *all* lives in *all* their diversity.

God is happy with nothing less and will support nothing else.

As the Creator, God has nothing to do with any human creation that in any way denies any of life's essentials to other creatures.

Supporting such human creations separates us from God's presence. We won't do it.

Day 51

When we are helpful to God in making all of life happy God will be give us our share in God's happiness.

Until then we will be stuck with creating our own happiness, which will be lower in quality and shorter in duration.

We begin to help God by changing how we treat the life right next to ours, right where we are, in the next 24 hours.
There is no other place to begin.
 There is no other time to begin.

If we can't add to the happiness of the life next to us we won't add to the happiness of those farther away.

We will bring the same indifferent blindness with us. Others will feel used, not helped.

Day 52

The first thing we do to make the life next to us happier is to stop doing harm.

We harm others by the things we do and say, and through the things we neglect to do and say.

Out of loyalty to God, we stop doing the things that harm another creature and start doing the helpful things we have been putting off.

We don't advertise what we did.

Trying to get attention and social approval for our good deeds is to sneak in a fee for our services. That fee keeps others from feeling the touch of God for themselves.

We would never do such a thing.

Day 53

Life already has a way of overcoming challenges and flourishing.

It was designed by the Author of Life.
It was there long before humanity evolved and will be there long after humanity is replaced.

Life's way is what God is teaching us.
The rest of nature already knows it.
We are playing catch up.
Our job is to learn Life's way and our role in it.

We are not completely free to determine what impulses we feel and what challenges we must overcome.

Much of that comes from our culture.
We are completely free to notice and reject behaviors that increase unhappiness on earth.

We begin to reject the culture.

Quietly at first, in the privacy of our own thoughts.

We then ask God for help to know what to do next.

Our role is to nurture what is already in us, put there by God.

When it is full and ripe God will show us how to freely distribute its richness in a unique way the culture can't comprehend.

We serve in such a way directs the attention of others toward God and creation, not toward ourselves or our group.

We have learned God meets our need for validity in a way that self-promotion can't.

Day 54

When we see evidence that someone has cultivated a gift from God we give them full credit they deserve for the work they do and the benefit they bring.

We don't want any more than what God has entrusted to us, but neither will we allow anyone to take it from us what is ours.

Give others the credit they are due, and they will be happy. Steal it and they will be unhappy.

To steal another's God-given happiness is to make ourselves enemies of God.

It is fearsome thing to be God's enemy.

Day 55

We are most likely to steal happiness from those we have power over.

In return God takes away ours.

It will not return until we return the happiness we have stolen.

God is just.

Day 56

You have been entrusted with a part of God's distributed happiness. Your part is to protect, nurture, and distribute it freely.

Your life exists to embody God's goodness in some way.

What have you been entrusted with?
Whatever you do easily and naturally, predictably produces results that benefit others.

Your calling is to work under God's supervision to fully develop what has been entrusted to you until you fully embody something beautiful and useful.

Give it time. Let it ripen.
God will make the most of your time on earth in ways you can't foresee.

Day 57

When we see life rich in variety working together, sharing a space and its resources without destructive conflict or waste – we have entered a place ruled by God.

Pay close attention to how things work in such a place.

Take special notice of what does not go on there.

Make sure those things do not go on in your life or work either.

Day 58

When we pay sustained attention to a thriving natural environment it becomes clear that God loves beauty.

Beauty is spontaneously organizing variety.

Where God rules we see ever more variety in ever more complex combinations.

Day 59

Variety is the spice of life!

A well-organized spice rack lets you easily and quickly try new recipes!

Imagine a spice rack that constantly grows and quickly rearranges itself as a new spice becomes available.

We move other spice jars around to make room for a new one.

It works the same way in a place ruled by God.

Day 60

There is a vast intelligence embedded in Creation.

Creation is its own designer and builder.
The Creator made it so.

As part of Creation, we too are made to design and build our own lives, individually and collectively.

It will be new, and it will fit the current set of needs.

We were not created to replicate another life, another time and another place fitted to another set of needs. We take our design direction from no other creature.

No other creature is God.

Day 61

You don't have anyone else's fingerprint.
You won't feel God's happiness trying to live out
someone else's life design.

God doesn't make copies.

The present is always made up of new and different
variables.

Our life design must constantly adapt to keep up, while
staying true to God's design for earth: more variety in
new, mutually beneficial combinations.

Day 62

Anything we see in nature is temporary.
The form we see is changing ever so slowly, sometimes quickly. Living things in nature respond to temporary circumstances by building temporary structures.

To participate in God's happiness, we too build and maintain temporary life structures. Trying to make our life structures permanent on a planet where everything else is temporary makes us the misfits on earth. It is a recipe for misery and causing misery.

We let go. We move on. We start again.
We are met and taught and helped by a vast intelligence.

A new, unfamiliar place and a new era in our lives converge to form a new beauty because of our guided creativity.

We learn to hold on tightly to God.

We learn to hold anything else loosely because it is just passing through our lives.

Day 63

We adapt to the changing situation individually as much as we can.

We do our most consequential adapting in groups.

God is most happy when a group is helpful to the design.

God is most unhappy when a group is harmful to the design.

We are a social species.
The most powerful capacity God gave us is the ability to work together for a common goal.

How we use that capacity is God's greatest concern.

As individuals we know God's happiness most when we are kind and constructive collectively.

We won't know God's happiness at all if our group is cruel and destructive and we do nothing about it.

Day 64

Most of the misery on earth that grieves God and harms nature is caused collectively, not individually.

If I stop adapting as soon as I am happier, if I have no concern for how my group behaves, I leave God's happiness.

I cannot accept the benefits of my group and at the same time deny or shrug off my group's harmful behaviors.

To belong to a group is to share the accountability for its behaviors.

I might come from an individualistic culture, but I was not created to be individualistic.

I was created to care for the whole, not just the part.

It is not all about me.

When I approach God thinking it is all about me, I meet a cold silence.

Day 65

God's happiness is different.

It grows mostly after we stop doing many things we
used to do and then start doing a few new things our
culture did not teach us to do.

Over time this new mix of behaviors alters the fragrance
of our lives. There are fewer painful emotions we carry
around with us and into everything we do.

Anxiety, anger, envy, bitterness, exhaustion, shame, and
despair make only temporary appearances, they no
longer define us.

Our load is lightened.
Our energy and attention are freed to attend to other
lives.

Day 66

What we do in the solitude of our hearts determines how happy we are.

Spending time alone is like approaching a mountain stream on a hot summer day. If there are no pollutants or pathogens in the water then it is refreshing and safe to drink.

However, if there are pollutants or pathogens in the water you have a real dilemma; you need water to survive, but you will get sick if you drink this water.

If it is your only source of water your body will not have the time to fight off the diseases before it is infected once again. You will be constantly sick and drained of energy.

So it is with our inner lives. In solitude God will systematically address and remove toxins from our social environment.

It is painful at first, but later we are happy it happened. We are refreshed and become a source of refreshment for the other lives around us.

Day 67

The most powerful toxins that ruin our happiness come
from the values and behaviors of the group we currently
belong to.

To remove them, God directs us to confront how our
group behaves, especially toward the innocent and
powerless.

If the group will not change, God directs us to leave the
group to find a new one. If there is none to be found
God will direct us to form a new one that will use its
capacity for collective action to increase the stock of
happiness on earth for all lives.

Either way, at some point we no longer carry the shame
of being part of a harmful group.
Instead, we carry a radiance on our faces.
Without words it reveals who we spend time with.

Day 68

There is a new lightness in God's happiness as we lug around fewer complaints.

There is a new brightness in God's happiness as we do fewer things that throw others into dark despair.

There is a new warmth in God's happiness as we shed our cold indifference to the suffering we were causing for others individually, or as part of a group.

There is a new clarity as God removes confusing, contradictory nonsense put in us from childhood by our culture, opening our field of view to see the wisdom of Creation.

Day 69

As God re-constructs us from the inside out, nature
starts to mean more to us.

We walk or run alone in nature.
We take our time.
We take it in.
We use all our senses.

As we go there frequently over the course of the year we
see things slowly change as the seasons change.

We are drawn deeper into the mysteries of Creation.

We uncover its wonders and recover a sense of
admiration and respect.

We become like whatever we admire.

Day 70

Creation is not anywhere near finished.
Its full potential has not even begun to appear.

We are here to participate in the unfolding of creation
and help it along.

Daily, under God's supervision.

God first directs us to observe, admire and learn from
nature for many, many years.

We must understand deeply what living things and
living systems do and need before we can be useful and
not harmful.

Day 71

God helps those who are helpful – to the ongoing work of creation.

God does not help those who help themselves and stop there.

God does not help a harmful group in any of its projects.

Day 72

We were created to be go-to problem solvers God can rely upon to do what needs to be done to further the divine design: growing variety sustained by growing cooperation.

God creates; we help.
Not the other way around.

We don't expect God to run errands for us.

We expect to run errands for God.

Day 73

The more time we spend with God the more responsive and pliable we become.

We notice the most subtle signals.

Our conscience alerts us faster that we are approaching an ethical limit to our actions.

Our curiosity alerts us to a creative possibility.

It all starts to become second nature.

It is fun and exciting.

Day 74

We start to instinctively look out for things God looks out for.

Increasingly we catch unhelpful attitudes and behaviors earlier before they become entrenched – in ourselves and in our group.

Unhelpful habits are much less painful to remove when they are addressed as soon as they show up.

Day 75

There was a time when pursuing happiness did not necessarily make us good to those around us.

When we were good it was often for show, to gain attention and admiration. We put on a good act, but backstage we were hurtful to others.

God's happiness re-purposes us. We no longer do good for show.

We become a flexible, vital component in a healthy, growing community of lives.

There is real goodness when there is no difference between our behaviors on-stage and back-stage.

Day 76

Real goodness requires no adoring audience to fuel or prove itself.

It is enough to know we are being watched by God while we care for God's creation.

Our actions in public will be reviewed tomorrow morning in private with God.

We want to grow closer to the standard modelled by nature.
No waste. Beautiful and useful.

We want our lives to embody the same vast intelligence we see in nature.

Day 77

Gods' happiness and God's goodness are two sides of the same coin.

Each replenishes the other daily, forged in situations when it seemed initially our happiness must come at the expense of someone else's happiness.

We stop. We ask for wisdom and guidance. We wait and listen.

The one who doesn't know waits on the one who does. It is the way we deal with any true authority.

God guides us until we find another way. We invent a new way.

Day 78

Seeking that better way becomes normal among us.

When something doesn't make sense we say so and don't go along with it.

When something doesn't work to increase the stock of happiness on earth we say so and won't go along with it.

We try to find out what is really going on, what is true. Then we run experiments until we find out what really works.

We constantly correct our understanding of what is true.

We constantly surpass the excellence we achieved before.

It is the way life does things.

Day 79

Using better answers and methods we grow the stock of happiness on earth, just as a wise gardener constantly enriches her soil.

Protest and reform create good social soil.

New kinds of good things will grow and combine with each other in that social soil bringing delight to God.

Blind acceptance of nonsense and custom leeches all truth and honor out of a society.

We do not submit to the dictatorship of the past, no matter how glorious it was supposed to be.

Nothing in nature does.
Why should we?

Day 80

The first soil we must recover is our own souls.

Sometimes what we *want* to do we *should not* do if we want to help make earth happier.

We go ahead and do what we want even though we are making earth a meaner place for another life.

Sometimes what we *don't want to do* is precisely what we *should do* to make the earth happier.

We ignore our conscience and put off doing what we know we should do.

Lazy neglect creates hurtful loneliness for others.

Those we neglect realize they are on their own.

When they ask for help nobody cares.
Nobody comes, even those who are supposed to care.

For as long as our neglect is causing life on earth to be hurtful to another, God's happiness will not catch up to us.

Day 81

There comes a day, years after we began to seek God, when what we *want* to do is exactly what we *should* do, and what we *don't want* to do is exactly what we *should not do.*

Where before our values and interests were at odds with each other, now they come together to complete each other.

The war inside ends.
There is peace.

We finally get restful sleep.

That is God's happiness catching up with us.

Day 82

How will I know if my interests and values are coming together?

When I can wait patiently.

A divided, complaining, discontented soul can't wait to get what it thinks will deliver happiness.

A grateful, contented soul can wait to pass on what it has been given in the best possible way to meet the need at hand.

Day 83

When God's happiness rules we will want to wait until it is possible to give the right thing, at the right time, for the right reason, to the right recipient, in the right way.

That may well take a lifetime!

Or longer. Sometimes the right recipient has not yet been born and the situation our work will meet has not yet unfolded.

Day 84

You may be gifted by God to create something that will only be appreciated long after your death.

Only God's happiness is sturdy enough to bear being ignored or even mocked for a lifetime, meeting death with confidence.

Enfolded in God's happiness we can calmly face death, having entrusted our contribution to God, who works in vast time scales.

Our contribution may come to fruition through the work of another who will pick up where we left off.

Day 85

Reversals happen in nature.

At some point in the winter the days stop getting shorter, darker, and colder.

They start getting longer, sunnier, and warmer. Spring is around the corner.

There comes a day when what we *want* to do energizes what we are *supposed* to do.

Frustration reverses to become disciplined play.

Despair reverses to become joy.

Bitterness reverses to become sweetness.

Weakness reverses into strength.

Day 86

Strength is not a huge pile of impressive capacities.

Strength is when all our capacities are pulling in the same direction, each multiplying the other.

Weakness is not a lack of impressive capacities.

Weakness is when our capacities are pulling against each other, cancelling each other out, causing exhaustion.

God's happiness is a strong happiness.

It makes us strong.

Day 87

To obtain happiness we used to start with what *we* wanted.

We got the idea from seeing an image of someone who appeared to have something we didn't have. We were just sure if we had it too we would be happy.

We weren't too concerned about what lives could get hurt in our pursuit of happiness.

After harming others and bearing the painful remorse a healthy soul feels afterwards, we learn not to pull in a different direction than where God wants us to go.

We stop working against God when we accept that The Creator does not make copies.

We learn that God's happiness does not join us when we attempt to become a modified version of someone else.

God's happiness only catches up to as we become what we alone were made to become.

Day 88

Remember, God's happiness is a *different* happiness, and it comes into our lives *differently*. God's happiness starts with what *God* wants, with what we are *obligated* to do.

We are an intelligent, observing, problem-solving, decision-making part of the earth's living system. We were given all those capacities, for free.

We are also given a calling. We enter a journey of exploration to find discover something to do with our capacities that harms no other life, something that adds to the total stock of happiness all lives can draw upon.

Head out in that direction and life gets interesting. It will not be a copy of anyone else's story.

Day 89

At some point in the summer, the days start getting shorter, the nights longer and colder. Winter is coming. No human, no matter how rich, famous, or powerful can reverse it or even slow it down.

Human endeavors that violate God's design will eventually slide from higher to lower order. It can't be stopped, reversed, or even slowed down for very long.

There are forgotten virtues from the past that rediscover, but there is no golden age we try to thaw out and re-heat.

Today is always a unique set of conditions. God doesn't do repeats. We pay attention here now, so we don't miss anything!

There are those who waste their lives trying to preserve something God is done with.

God is endlessly creative and has something far better in mind, something that has never yet been.

Day 90

At some point in the winter the days start getting longer, the nights shorter.
Spring is coming.

No human activity can stop it or slow it down. And it will not be a copy of last Spring.

There will be new varieties and arrangements. The specifics can't be predicted.

There is no utopia ahead where there will be no struggle or loss. There is no grand design we can know ahead of time.
We are not God.

God's new design emerges daily in response to a set of circumstances that has never existed before. We go with it, making sure the lives we touch get their full share of God's goodness.

Day 91

The unfolding of God's design is like hearing a wonderful piece of music for the first time. A musical performance usually starts with written music. There is a design.

Right now, the music exists only on paper and in the mind of the composer. But it does not stay there. There is a process by which the design unfolds into an enveloping, living experience.

It is a form of disciplined play.

To start, every musician or singer focuses on the same piece of music, usually in private.

Each works alone, but with the others in mind. Each learns their own part. They see when they join in and when they don't.

The musicians get an abstract sense of how it fits together before they experience it, but they have learned the actual experience playing together will be so much richer than they can imagine alone.

When the time comes to play together the first thing they do is tune their instrument to the same tone as everyone else.

Next, every musician adjusts their timing to play to the same beat.

There are many more steps and refinements.

When it all comes together, after much individual and group practice – it is one of the best experiences we can share as humans, next to breaking bread together.

Day 92

It is wonderful to behold a thriving community of lives coming together to do something none of them could have done alone.

Each type benefits from the presence of the other. Just like the instruments in a musical group, they aren't all alike.

They don't always agree.

It is not all sweet all the time. There are dissonant notes and minor keys.

Seeing how differences join into a useful whole over time is a big part of what makes it all so rich and satisfying. It is the clearest evidence God is welcome and active in our midst.

Day 93

When we hear music we like for the first time each note is new, but somehow no other note would have worked as well.

It is just as it should be. We wouldn't change a thing. Even the dark parts.

In a musical masterpiece there is no wasted note which added nothing to the experience. There is no note missing that needed to be there for it all to work.

There are pauses when silence carries the mood. When it all comes together the piece perfectly performs its function to bring us to a different place emotionally.

A creation of any kind is perfect when it fully performs its intended function.

That is not to say it is flawless. Perfect does not mean flawless. Something is perfect that meets a real need when and where the need appears.

If my jacket is the right weight for the conditions outside it is perfect. It doesn't matter if it has a tear on the sleeve or a missing button.

Day 94

No living thing is perfect that did not make mistakes along the way. There is no creature that did not fail to fully function for some time. We struggle our way through, with help. There is no other way.

It is precisely our mistakes, failures and imperfections that make us authentic, relatable, and approachable. It is the fact that we struggled to overcome the ways in which we once hurt others that makes it normal for others to do the same.

In God's happiness we learn with and from each other, especially from each other's struggles. Each of us gets to learn something without having to pay the full price the other paid, simply by imitating what they learned to do differently after failing.

Day 95

God has no need for a people who have never struggled or failed, who think they know everything and look down on the rest of us.

Such behavior has ruined God's name and turns mentioning God in public into a mark of ignorance and bigotry.

God's name had to be ruined first before humans felt free to ruin God's creation.

Day 96

Our job is to restore the honor of God's name.

Then and only then can the work of restoring Earth really work the way it is supposed to.

Then and only then will humans do the work under God's wise direction - *together*.

Without God limiting our individual and group selfishness we can't work together, no matter how important the cause or urgent the crisis.

When we live and work apart from God's ethical correction we will predictably fail each other the most at the very moment we need each other the most.

Day 97

God does not expect you to be flawless. There is no such creature. God promises no creature on earth there will be no pain, injury, or loss.
Every creature, no matter how magnificent, carries blemishes, scars, and the antibodies of severe diseases it once fought off.

What God does expect is for you to grow into completeness so you can fulfill your unique part of the design for Earth. What God does promise is to be with you through all the hard things of life. It is your struggle to deal with those things that proves God's faithfulness and power is available to us all, through anything, no matter what.

We don't seek God expecting ease. We seek God expecting work and to be re-worked until, over time, we become more unique and more complete.

Day 98

Uniqueness and completeness unfold only in the lives of those who seek God first and want most to be helpful.

Our guided unfolding helps complete God's design for earth.

Life on earth unfolds over a vast expanse of time. It moves, changes, flows, combines, and evolves. The unfolding never stops, repeats itself or stalls.

We are part *of* Earth; we are not apart *from* it.
Our lives individually and in groups unfold in the same way as everything else on Earth,
     through struggling to adjust to the situation at hand.

How could it be otherwise?

Day 99

We don't toss God our leftover scraps of time, attention, and ability.

We don't soothe our conscience with cheap rituals or token contributions to a worthy cause or institution.

We used to do that. We thought we had bought off God for a week so we could go back to treating others anyway we wanted as we pursued what we were just sure would make us happy.

We realize now how deeply insulting that behavior is to God. It guaranteed the absence of God in our lives.

Dead religion often lies at the heart of cruelty and indifference.

Day 100

As created residents of earth, the Creator gave us a home that sustains our lives. We did not create that home and could not replace it if lost. We don't live in debt to God and don't see God as a cosmic creditor.

We live in love with God and naturally want to participate in whatever our Beloved is up to. The way we get to join the work is to bring the best we've got to God and seek direction on how to make the most of it.

We set aside our best rested time, energy, and attention to meet with God. In this way we prepare to meet the new day God has given us. We know we may not get another.

We give our best because more than anything *on* earth we want to contribute to what *God wants* most *for* earth.

God's direction ensures that what we do does not interfere with life's processes, leaving it poorer and weaker.

Rather, God directs our actions in such a way that our unique contributions interact with and enrich life.

Day 101

We commit ourselves to something larger and greater than ourselves.

We live out that commitment in our daily, practical activities.

We freely choose to give our best to further what God wants most.

We don't think solemn rituals or inspiring shows substitute for helpful living. There has been no shortage of either over the course of human history.

If rituals and shows haven't made us behave better by now a new one isn't going to work either.

What God wants from us is something new and different, not a copy or new version of what has failed to bring peace and justice to earth.

Day 102

What God wants most is beyond any personal dream, beyond the interests of any one group or any one species.

To stop at any of those goals is to leave God's work undone and to abandon God's protection, provision, and direction. It is to miss out on all the miracles.

We don't stop at a place where God's happiness will pass us by, no matter how pleasant that place is, no matter how proud we are of what we have done.

We visit pleasant places temporarily. God gives times of refreshment. We reach high places through struggle.

God gives moments of brilliant clarity.

Then it is time to move on.

We learn that when we try to make permanent what is temporary, we lose the company of those who are truly helpful.

Those who chase and hoard thrilling experiences are different from those who seek to be helpful to God.

Helping another in need is often not thrilling. So those who chase peak spiritual experiences will not show up to help. They are useless in a time of need.

We leave the company of spiritual thrill seekers and keep moving because we never want to find ourselves on our own, without God and without the help of truly helpful people.

Day 103

A composer does not care most about only one note, or the part for one voice or instrument.
The composer cares most about the whole composition.

The whole explains why the parts exist.
Each part helps complete the whole.

God designed life to be meaningful. It is very meaningful the more we understand and fulfill our part in the whole.

Otherwise, it has no lasting meaning.

Only God knows what the whole is to become and how we can best help. It is one of those things where you just *had* to *be there.*

YOU just had to be there. No one else would do.

Day 104

The Great Composer starts re-working our lives by directing our attention to our obligations to the lives who directly depend upon us.

It is like having the musical score set before us. We are unable to even begin to play parts of it with any skill or enjoyment.
That is normal.

The gap between what we are obliged to do and what we can do causes frustration. That frustration is like a charged battery. It stores up energy to fuel us through the challenging work ahead.

We don't seek a quick release from that frustration. We accept it as a necessary tension. Someday we will be so glad we did not run away to chase something easier and faster.

Day 105

We start to see God's design unfold in and around us.

We realize it is a good thing that we are not like other people.

Our gifts fit situations that their gifts can't.

We could not have anticipated the situations God would fit us to because those situations did not exist until now.

Those situations explain why we needed to be different, why our story needed to be different.

It all fits.

Day 106

What we thought were flaws, when re-purposed by God, become assets.

In our cruel losses we came to love the One who alone can restore and replace.

We calm down.

The better we fit the situation the fewer fits of anxiety, rage, and despair we have inside.

We stop making ourselves so miserable.

Day 107

The better we fit the situation we throw fewer fits around others.

We stop making others so miserable.

We can accept and appreciate ourselves in ways we could not before. Those around us can accept and appreciate us in new ways as well.

It is in silence and solitude that long festering wounds heal.

It happens faster the more often we can be alone with God outside in nature.

A new fruitfulness awaits.

Day 108

As we go about our normal activities, we give a voice to the voiceless. We defend the defenseless and innocent.

We do not stand by and do nothing.
We speak up to protect the God-given rights of newcomer and stranger.

Sometimes expanding God's happiness on earth puts us in the way of our own group as it pursues its exclusive notions of happiness.
We risk our standing within our own group to protect those God cares about, but who our group ignores.

All evil begins with ignoring. The best time to stop evil is right when it starts, in the planning stage.

At no time do we need God's guidance more.

Day 109

We choose not to ignore the whisper, the touch from God. It is in that ignoring, in that lifeless soil, all evil first takes root.

We seek God's wisdom in silence and solitude. God meets and equips us for the struggle ahead, daily, all the way through the conflict we find ourselves part of.

We have been helpful in furthering God's design. We have taken sides. We stand *on* God's side and identify with God's interests.
God wants both sides to thrive, but not at each other's expense.

That is God's justice.

We stay *by* God's side, quiet enough to keep hearing that wise whisper, tender enough to keep feeling that caring nudge.

God guides us to take our place beside the ignored and despised.

God does not give us words until and unless the situation requires words.

In return, we God does not ignore us and our concerns.

God meets and helps in ways we could not have foreseen.

God intervenes in the situation, creating an opening.

We step into the opening and contend for the true well-being of all involved.

Day 110

There are limits to our knowledge. Even connected to God's guidance, beyond a certain point we can't be certain what will happen because of our actions.

No creature knows the future, only The Creator does.

We learn to spot the line of uncertainty. Beyond that line lies the domain of God. Only God can foresee unintended consequences. Only God foresees events that can derail our plans. Only God knows the real intentions of others we interact with. Only God knows our own conceits – when we are misleading ourselves.

We stop at the line of uncertainty and do what other creatures in nature do. We call out. We send out a signal requesting assistance:

HELP!

Day 111

We ask for help anytime we can't know for certain what is really going on and how things will turn out.

Then we fall silent, listen, watch, and wait.

God meets us and calms us. We listen. God teaches and corrects us. We have not ignored God. We have not crossed lines God told us not to cross.

Unlike those who ignore God's concerns, God does not ignore our calls.

God answers.

God comes alongside and gently prepares us to act with care and precision when the opportunity presents itself.

God presents that opportunity by altering the situation in an unforeseen way, making something possible that was impossible only hours before.

We move into the opportunity with calm, measured, competence.

It is our note to play and our time to play it.

Our precise, controlled response to the unique situation demonstrates God's wisdom.

Our attitude and behaviors in that moment convey God's concern for all the lives involved.

It changes the situation into one far richer in possibilities, and far better than anything anyone could have planned.

Day 112

God wants us to learn how to get the most benefit from periods of solitude.

You will find the farther you move toward God's happiness the less company you will have.

You don't need to wait until you have company to get underway. You will have company. You will live in the presence of God. Nature will be your teacher.

Your longing for others to also know God's presence and share in the work will never wane. God wants that too.

Others need someone to follow into God's presence. That someone in today's situation may be you.

Day 113

Loneliness is not the lack of company. Loneliness is the lack of good company.

Good company consists of those who collaborate with you to create a relationship that is equally beneficial, and more.

The relationship meets your needs, their needs, and helps construct what God desires for earth, a place where such relationships are normal.

A mutually beneficial relationship is reciprocal. You receive as much as you give. You cut each other's burdens in half by bearing them together. You double each other's joys by celebrating each other's victories.

There will be periods when the only one who behaves this way is God. (Besides your dog if God placed one in your life.)

Day 114

A constant source of unhappiness is comparison.

We compare ourselves to others and come up lacking. We feel envy and resentment.

As we grow closer to God we learn to assess the success of our lives differently.

Instead of focusing on what we got or didn't get, we focus on how we behave or don't behave.

We ask whether the way we behave brings joy to God by increasing the stock of happiness on earth.

Day 115

Envy is a mirage. Comparing ourselves to others is a trap.

It is not possible to close the gap between the life we get to live, and the life others get to live.

It is possible to close the gap between how we live now and how God designed us to live our unique, one and only life. The gap *will* close If we live in constant contact with God's directing, correcting signal.

It is as inevitable as the coming of spring.

As we become more like what God designed us to become, we will feel the smile of God.

We will be glad we became no one else, living no other life than the one given to us, with all its challenges.

In God's happiness, contentment replaces envy.

Day 116

Tedium is the sign that we are on a path headed *down* to a state of stagnation.

Tantrums are a sign we are on a path headed *down* to a state of chaos.

We find God's happiness only on a path headed *up* to a state of higher ordered complexity. God's helpers are rigorous and vigorous. We are unflappable but not inflexible. We accept high standards, and the struggle required to live up to them.

We have disciplines that keep us lively and energetic so we can continue the struggle as long as it takes.

There is joy in the high places that does not exist in low places.

Day 117

Sliding lower faster on slippery places is easy and fun for a while. The way it ends is awful and irreversible.

Climbing slowly higher is hard and frustrating for extended periods of time. Then, suddenly there are openings near the peak, stunning beyond words. We are bathed in the glory of God.

There is nothing like it amid the noisy crowd.

Pain and exhaustion are forgotten, replaced by awe and overflowing joy.

We know first-hand the miracles of reversal and replacement.

We participate in the arrival of the new and better.

Day 118

We are God's workers.

God is the best employer on earth.

Our relationship to God is a working relationship.

Very few things can make us more miserable, make us feel more alone, than a bad job.

God creates the best jobs on earth.

There is nothing more interesting, more satisfying, more rewarding than participating productively in the ongoing work of creation.

Day 119

Only working together can forge a true friendship.

To know if someone is truly cooperative, we must first see them work, see their work, or talk to someone who has seen them work.

A person's work habits and work product reveal the truth about their intentions and ethics.

Trying to get something done with someone who is selfish or lazy is like running on a broken ankle.

Day 120

Following God's ethical signal makes our work effective over time.

True work that works is the use of time and energy to change a situation from what it was into something that functions at a higher level.

If the situation doesn't change, our work isn't working. If it changes temporarily and then slides right back to what it was, our work isn't working. If in our efforts to make things better we end up making things worse, our work isn't working.

There is nothing more disheartening than to see a life's work crumble and vanish.

That does not happen when we labor under God's direction. Something remains and lives into the future, setting in motion things that would not have happened otherwise.

Day 121

We do nothing that interferes with God's direction.

For example, we don't attempt to make exclusive deals with God for ourselves or our group.

We don't try to get something from God our culture says will make us happy by promising to give something in return.

We have no standing to do such a thing. It assumes we know best, and God doesn't, which is an insult to The Creator.

Do you like spending time alone with someone who insults you?

Day 122

Deal-making can only occur between equals.

Those who try to make deals with God seem to think they are equal to The Creator.

There is no comparison between a finite mortal and the Infinite Eternal Creator.

Those who approach God trying to strike a deal find nothing.

The voice they imagine they hear is only the voice of their fantasies.

It comes from envy and leads to emptiness.

Day 123

We also interfere with God's direction when we try to make God do what we want using secret techniques.

Magic is trying to direct The Creator's unlimited power to create some kind of private fantasy in which life is composed of all pleasure with no pain, all gain with no loss, all ease with no struggle, all praise with no criticism.

It is the worldview of a two-year-old. Just as two-year-olds think they are greater than their parents and should be in charge, magicians imagine they are greater than God.

Magical thinking never turns out well because it breaks the mind's contact with reality and hardens' the heart's attitude toward it.

There is no secret that shows us how to take the place of God.

The reason is simple; as long as...

We can't make something out of nothing...
We can't turn non-living materials in to living creatures...
We can't predict the future...
We can't be everywhere at once...
We can't know everything....

We are nowhere near equal with God.

We certainly are not greater.

Out of profound respect for the Creator, we reject magic and avoid those who practice it.

Day 124

Fantasies come from fiction and advertising. Those who produce fiction and advertising have their own agenda. They benefit immediately when you buy their products.

Your benefit is supposed to come later.

The way to know something is a fantasy is it starts with "If only..."

Fantasy presumes a set of conditions that don't exist, never have and never will.

From there we imagine our own personal or group utopia.

Any fantasy is a mirage.

When we arrive at the place happiness is supposed to be, it is not there. Or it is there but doesn't live up to the promise. The promised happiness has moved off into the distance and now you must make another sacrifice to catch up with those who are supposedly happy.

It is a cruel joke.

We will be cruel to those who get in our way any time we chase fantasies.

We create pain for others in our pursuit of a life without pain.

What makes that ok?

Day 125

God has high standards but is not cruel.
God will do nothing to help fulfill our fantasies, either
personally or collectively.

God's happiness flows out of our direct contact with
what is real, verifiable, and observable. We don't have
to take anyone else's word for it.

As we use our own eyes, ears and reasoning, God
teaches us to do quiet things that will reliably increase
the stock of happiness on earth. But it does not happen
fast. We must learn patience.

To onlookers, the change in our tone demonstrates
God's presence, wisdom, and competence, not ours.

Over time, living this way, the situation changes into
something far better than any scene from fantasy or
fiction.

We would be the first to acknowledge how pivotal
God's direction and intervention was in changing the
situation for the better.

Day 126

When we do the things fantasy and fiction enticed us to do we inevitably end up putting on shows and playing win/lose games. It does nothing to increase the stock of happiness on earth, while burning up time and resources.

Unguided endeavors don't work reliably or for long. Usually, they cause more problems than they solve.

We never tie God's name to such activities.

Instead, we start where we are and do what is just regarding the lives around us.

It may not look like much but the fact that it is happening at all, in the absence of any attention or reward, reveals there is a power at work great enough to change a human heart at its core.

Who else can do that but God?

Day 127

When you receive and follow God's directing signal, you will behave in ways those around you can't or won't.

Acting decisively without fanfare, but with wisdom and justice, speaks more eloquently than words.

Like a splinter in the mind, your guided behavior creates a memory that others can't ignore or remove.

Others wonder, what is going on inside you that you do the right thing with no hope of recognition or reward?

It may take decades, but that nagging question will do its work in at least one other soul.

Day 128

We find the thing we can do to make a difference right where we are. We use what God have us. We affect the lives we already share space with. We improve the experience we share with others in that space.

A little bit of the world gets a little happier.
Or at least a little less cruel.
Right where we are the vast intelligence of God unfolds before our eyes in the low, the small and the overlooked.

We don't need to go to exotic places and be around exotic people to reach the high places where stunning vistas unfold. That is a fantasy. If that were the case only those with money could participate. Only a cruel god would set things up that way.

We look away from such gods.

Day 129

False gods are recognizable by their cruelty, hidden behind luxury.

Cultures with a cruel god become cruel, especially to their most vulnerable members.

If we become a cruel people it is because we first created a cruel god. If we become consistently cruel we forfeit our right to space on earth as a species.

Our extinction will be the natural consequence of our own selfishness.

We will have brought it on ourselves.

Day 130

Money, fame, pleasure, and power are cruel gods. Carefully study any person or society that lived in the service of these monsters. Don't trust the reports from their paid publicists.
Wait until a good objective history comes out.

Writing advertising copy is fast and easy and is the opposite of writing reliable history.
Writing objective history is a slow, patient forensic process, not unlike what police officers do at a crime scene.

Eventually the true story always comes out and reveals that the rich, powerful, and famous sacrificed the innocent to get their prize.
They gave up their integrity, their relationships, their safety, and sanity to gain the fleeting smile of their false god, only to have a rival take them down using the same methods.

Day 131

The true God is kind.

As temporary residents of earth we are privileged to receive, multiply, and pass on God's kindness in ways no other creature can.

Our unique abilities to use language and tools allow us to make sure all creatures live out the purpose of their existence.

In so doing we live out the purpose of our existence.

What a life!

Day 132

When God prevents you from pursuing a fantasy it is out of protective kindness.

Go ahead and pout for a while.

But accept God's "NO" as from a greater mind who loves you and truly knows best.

Fantasies come from advertising and unhelpful fiction. There is helpful fiction, but it is rarer than unhelpful fiction.

God will never meet and direct you through advertising or unhelpful fiction. Those venues make it all too easy to cleverly sneak in falsehoods and half-truths.

The mix of truth and error is as deadly as the mix of water and arsenic.

Day 133

God will direct you through disciplines that constantly find and remove false information while seeking to fill in gaps to make their information as complete as currently possible.

The disciplines of history and natural science have mechanisms that constantly update and correct previous errors through the discovery of new evidence, and through spirited debate.

Unhelpful fiction and advertising never correct previous errors.

Day 134

As we become more aware of the suffering of others caused by our behavior, our conscience will also constantly update and correct our social habits. Here helpful fiction can play a limited role.

Fiction is helpful when it encourages turning our attention to God. Many of our ethical choices take decades to play out. By that time, it is too late to go back and make a different choice.

Fiction can compress the story of decades into something short enough to show us ahead of time how a godless act can destroy life, or how a life guided by God can encourage life.

Fiction can be very helpful in the ethical development of children. Fiction can store and keep alive the longing for a just society.

Fiction that teaches us to fear the justice of God is helpful.

Fiction can be a pleasant supplement for adults, but we don't make it our main source of direction and inspiration. God have us history and nature for that. As sources they are more dependable because in fact-based disciplines there is less opportunity or temptation for a writer to treat wishes and dreams as facts.

As adults we carry the responsibility for others so reality must predominate. We must come to terms with stubborn facts.

In time our own lives become stubborn facts for others to acknowledge as they see our guided choices play out very differently than theirs over decades.

Day 135

Follow what you get from reliable, factual sources, and God's guiding signal will grow stronger and clearer.

God's signal will always imbed itself in information verified through observation, logic, and experiments. With reliable information we can see choices and their consequences, causes and their effects and choose our actions accordingly.

Ignore what is available through reliable sources at your peril.

Every moment we spend focusing on unreliable sources and unverifiable stories is time spent losing our ability to receive God's signal through reliable sources.

What we use grows. What we don't use shrinks.

Day 136

God will never use the enticement of material luxury to capture your attention and guide your actions. The love of luxury grows as the love of God wanes.

Conversely, the more empathetic we are about the suffering of others the less we will want to wallow in or parade our privilege.

It will just feel wrong.

The key to the question of luxury is helpfulness. How does this luxury item help grow the stock of happiness for all life on earth?

Is its purpose to increase the happiness of its owner more than anyone else? Does it function to create envy among those who can't afford it?

Does it create the impression God gives a few people significantly more than they need and everyone else significantly less than they need?

Does making and delivering it destroy living systems somewhere far away using labor paid too little to survive?

Material luxury is a visible form of hoarding.
It is a substitute for joy.

When you see luxury you can be sure invisible suffering
is in the mix somewhere, making the luxury item or
experience possible.

True luxury is the time to be quiet and alone with God
in nature, which leads to joy. True luxury does not
cause suffering for any other life.

Day 137

God may place money, power, recognition, or comforts in the situation of your birth. The point is not to try to get more.

These resources are a means, not an end in themselves. The more resources God entrusts to you the more God will hold you accountable how well you use them.

Receiving more than others is no reason to gloat or lord it over others. It is a reason to seek God's direction even more than those who received less.

Day 138

God may place little money, power, recognition, or pleasure in your life. The point is not to get more. The point is to get enough by making the most of what God have you.

Show yourself worthy for God to entrusted you with opportunity. Then watch for the opportunity to be helpful. When it appears, know it is an assignment from God. Make the most of it.

Truly helpful people are rare and can often command higher pay than those who are unhelpful.

Receiving little at birth is not a reason to accuse God, envy others or to demand that others pay your way. Under God's guidance you can turn a little into more, more than it takes to meet your own needs. Those you love will benefit too.

Day 139

Guided by selfishness, any fool can turn a lot into a little.

A lot of trust, goodwill, cooperation, and helpfulness is better than a lot of stuff.

It is a rare person who can turn a little into a lot.

Guided by God you can be that person.

You can be a model for all the others who receive little at birth.

They can reliably follow your example to a better life.

Day 140

God's happiness starts with a warmup exercise that may last as long as decade.

We learn to be happy *without* the things the world promised would make us happy.

We learn what not to do.
We stop chasing those things because they block out God's signal.
We must silence those distractions first.

Then comes the big lesson.

We can only be truly happy *with* another, in a mutually beneficial relationship – with God, with nature, with those right next to us. Not with non-living things we possess and control.

Day 141

Who are you with?

What is it like to do anything with you?

Whose benefit are you working for when you work together on something?

Everyone around you already knows the answers to these questions!

We are often the last to see it.

Day 142

If my time in solitude is all about me I am alone. I am far from God.

When I am *with* myself only and *for* myself only I leave the community of life. It may be cozy and comfortable, I may feel smug and superior, but at some point it all becomes tedious and predictable. My pursuit of pleasure harms others as I run over them or ignore them in pursuit of my own personal fantasy.

Life with God is not cozy and comfortable, but neither is it tedious, predictable, or harmful to others.

By struggling to keep pace with God, dealing with reality, we grow and grow and stimulate healthy growth around us.

Day 143

At times we God provides no other human to live with, sharing the same space.

Yet in those times we can still be with a plant, an animal, and our shared Creator – daily.

Do we keep the living things around us healthy and happy?

If so it won't be long until they reciprocate and add to our health and happiness in delightful and unexpected ways.

God invites us back into the community of Life.

Day 144

If we live alone we will still share moments with a neighbor, a co-worker, a store clerk, a landlord, a repair person, or a friend.

How are we "with" them? Complaining? Suspicious? Scolding? Mocking? Controlling? Attention-seeking? Ignoring? Neglecting? Bragging? Argumentative? Interrupting? Condescending?

We learn to see the experience we are creating for others by the way we typically behave.

It may come as a shock. God has seen it all along and is not happy. Feeling guilty at that moment is healthy. It is the awakening of conscience, one of the three reliable sources of guidance.

Day 145

Conscience is there to make sure we don't behave in harmful ways again.

Guilt protects us from causing further injury to another life, in the same way that a tender bruise keeps us from injuring ourselves in that place again.

We poorly protect what we cannot see or feel. God lets us feel the pain we cause others so we will be more protective of them next time.

The pain of conscience motivates us to ask God to help us to replace hurtful social habits with helpful ones.

We don't dispel our guilt by doing unrequested nice things later. We learn to stop doing hurtful things in the first place.

Day 146

If you can't physically touch another creature, if another creature cannot physically touch you, you are not really *with* that life, whether it be a plant or an animal.

Without real contact you really don't know that creature, it can't really interact with you. A fellow creature is one that *can* see your responses and adjust its own next moves because of what you did.

If there is no immediate, mutual change in behavior you are relating to an image.
We learn nothing about God's happiness relating to any image of any kind.

No fictional character or celebrity can function as a fellow creature in our daily lives, nor can anything made of stone.

Day 147

God has placed living fellow creatures in your path.

Notice them. See them. Hear them.

Respond to their responses by modifying your own. This is the way we grow ethically because it is in managing a living relationship that God meets us and changes us in ways we can't plan or engineer.

As relationships become primary, fiction and fantasies start to lose their charm. You won't want to control others; you will want to learn with and from them, give to and receive from them, laugh and cry with them.

Your own life becomes the most interesting story you have encountered.

Day 148

We all need stories to make sense of our world.

We learn to find stories that help us see and understand reality, not ones designed as an escape from reality.

We don't live vicariously through others, real or imagined.

We don't need to.

We no longer want to escape or control reality.

We are no longer content being spectators.

We want nothing else and nothing less than to enter the flowing, changing, unpredictable story of Life.

Day 149

Beware of productions that substitute for real relationships. Substitutes grow and come to replace the real thing. They can't hurt you directly. But they can't help you directly either.

Substitutes typically put on a safe show for you, for a fee. By focusing on them you will only learn how to put on a show for others, for a fee. The fee is sometimes monetary, but it always involves admiration and praise.

We then come to expect admiration for how wonderful we are when we put on a show.

Mutual flattery blocks out God's signal. Pride and selfishness take its place and pretend to be the voice of God.

Day 150

People direct flattery at a person, saying the whole package is wonderful.

Only God can make that assessment because only God knows the thoughts and intentions of any person.

When we flatter we cross the line and claim God's privilege as own's own.

To know God's happiness, we learn not to flatter or seek flattery.

Day 151

Encouragement is different from flattery. We direct encouragement at a person's specific behavior. We encourage another person when we point out a specific deed and how it meets the need of the situation.

We express both admiration for the skill used and gratitude for how helpful it is. Encouragement makes it normal to contribute to the well-being of others. To know God's happiness, we learn to always encourage specific helpful behavior.

Someone who has never met you, someone famous and far away, cannot encourage you in the same way.

An imaginary relationship is no substitute for a real one.

Day 152

Rather than focusing on those far away who do not share our situation, we turn our attention to the fellow creatures who do share our situation.

It is in our unrehearsed responses to them that we see evidence of growth, or not. So will others, especially when we feel hurt and angry.

It is true that real people can hurt you while celebrities and fictional or historical characters can't.

But The Divine Presence is closed to those who are not learning through trial and error to treat the real lives around them well.

Day 153

No ritual or ceremony, no canned and planned cathartic experience, no mind-altering drug, no secret chant, can open the door to The Divine Presence.

Those packaged experiences, purchased for a fee, only soothe our conscience while leaving us locked outside. Packaged, mood-altering experiences mask the underlying disease that is only getting worse.

Far from public displays, there are a few quiet souls who just keep becoming less harmful and more helpful to Life, daily.

These alone are invited to meet the Author of Life.

It is only fair.

Day 154

Unlike flatterers, God will never give us the impression we have arrived at enlightenment and perfection because no creature exists in nature which has arrived at enlightenment and perfection – none of us.

God designed all living things to self-correct and self-exceed. In nature creatures correct and replace behaviors that are not well suited to the emerging situation with ones better suited to the future.

Whatever was once excellent was excellent because of how well it fit the need of the times, not because it copied something from the past endlessly.

Our excellence must exceed what was excellent in the past because our situation has moved on.

Day 155

Our immune system works to heal us of diseases and equips our bodies to quickly recognize and throw off the same disease again next time it comes around.

Those who constantly self-correct and self-exceed are permitted to live in God's presence. They become carriers of God's healing happiness by representing God's interests on earth. They embody God's ethics in the way they treat any life they encounter.

Any social system we encounter that does not quickly self-correct and never exceeds its past glories is far from God. We will not find God's happiness there.

God does not run museums and does nothing irrelevant in today's situation.

Day 156

As agents of God's happiness, with a plant or animal, we are attentive, protective, and gentle.

If a creature is dependent upon us to survive, we never neglect its needs.

With another human, we listen more than we talk.

We don't attempt to put on a show to impress others any more than we would try to put on a show to impress a plant or a dog.

Day 157

When others are trying to tell us something we don't interrupt, we don't change the subject.

We let them finish.
If it is important to them it is important.

We ask questions and listen to the answers without interrupting.

We never learn anything when we are talking, only when we are listening. We can't know ahead of time the importance of what we will hear. Others will often begin with something that seems trivial, testing to see how attentive we are. We hear them.

We show interest and ask non-intrusive follow-up questions we could not ask had we not paid attention so far.

Day 158

God brings out in us the natural manners of those made to work in the chambers of the highest court.

Under the gaze of the highest authority, we develop habits of exquisite courtesy.

We give attention, we don't seek attention. When we listen, we take notes.
All good listeners take notes.

We don't yell or use vulgar language. We don't need to. We have other ways of getting a point across.

We don't ignore people. We acknowledge their presence. We make eye contact.

We greet others by name, warmly with a smile.

Day 159

We openly admire anything useful another person can do.

We know we are seeing a gift God gave them. To honor their skill is to honor God.
We express appreciation for the beneficial actions of others.

We quickly acknowledge any harmful act or omission on our part, whether it was accidental or intentional, then take action to make it right.

We are gracious and kind, not argumentative. We de-escalate conflicts. We settle disputes quickly and fairly. We are cooperative, looking for ways to work with others toward mutually beneficial objectives.

Day 160

With at least one approachable neighbor, an agent of God's happiness makes the neighborhood a safer, happier, less lonely place. We become part of what makes home feel like home.

With at least one approachable co-worker an agent of God's happiness makes the workplace fun, nimbler, and more productive. We become part of what makes work rewarding.

We can't fully see the experience we are creating, but we can see that it matters to people. It is uncommon and valuable.
It is life giving. When God's agents are absent others notice because everything is harsher and less interesting.

It is harder to get anything done or done well.

Day 161

Our own intimate relationship with God often begins in an appeal to a higher authority because we had no place else to go.

We felt misjudged by those in power and there was no human court of appeal to set the record straight.

We brought our case directly to God, the highest authority whose word is final.

God met and heard us in our pain. It was our first taste of the Creator's kindness and justice.

We learned to see our part in what happened and what not to do again.

We came to see that what harmed us unfairly is out there harming others unfairly.

To our surprise God asked us to do something about what is harming life on earth, since we understand it personally.

We accepted the assignment.

Now we are agents of God's appeals court.

Our courtly behaviors send a signal to others that God has not gone out of business as they have been told.

The Divine court is open, and justice will be served. Wrongs will be righted. Nature itself will join the battle on our side for it too has been wronged.

There will be no rescue for those who stand in the way.

Along with good manners we exude calm confidence. We know who is going to win.

Day 162

Never confuse the courtly manners of the godly with being "nice."

Niceness alone is not enough when goodness must confront evil.

It is easy to be strong and bad.
The evil never wrestle with their conscience because they killed it long ago. They simply envision a situation in which they get everything they want and then trample the innocent who happen to get in the way.

God takes notice. There will be natural consequences, set in motion by the deed itself. When the consequences arrive, they cannot be reversed. God will deny their appeal.

The evil will have no place to go and no place to hide.

Day 163

It is also easy to be good and weak.
Good weaklings use lofty words but don't stand up and
speak out on behalf of the innocent and powerless.
They never oppose the strong and bad in a way that
does anything to stop them.

Good weaklings often claim the name of God while
doing nothing.
God takes notice.

There will be natural consequences, set in motion by
their refusal to risk their standing, comfort and ease.
Evil waits to make sure "good people" will do nothing.

The cowardice and passivity of the "good" gives the evil
permission and encouragement to do more harm than
ever before.

Day 164

The institutions of the weak good lose all moral standing and vanish from history.

That is one reason we turn to history to become more attuned to God's ethical signal. We learn to spot the moves of a weak good organization.

We don't repeat what failed in the past.

God will not protect weak good organizations, so we don't waste our time working for them or working to save them.

Instead, we move on.

We learn at the expense of those who went before us and struggle to find a better, stronger way to respond in moments of moral crisis.

Day 165

It is very difficult to be strong and good.
Strong goodness is what God's happiness creates in
time, in both individuals and groups.

The ability to stay under control ethically and
emotionally, especially in conflict situations that require
decisive action - is as rare as it is valuable.

Our self-control is proof of an internal strength gained
in the service of the highest authority on earth.

Our self-control certifies that the actions we take in a
conflict are being actively guided by the highest
authority.

Strong goodness shows up in the rare ability to work
together see a noble purpose through in the face of
opposition, loss, set-back and adversity, even if it takes
generations.

God takes notice and deploys all of nature to intervene
decisively in the struggle.

History records the verdict and describes the sentence

imposed on those who refused God's direction and correction.

The memory of the honorable will be preserved.

The harmful will cease to exist at all.

God gives the weasels and wobblers in between another chance but does not promise more than one chance to choose. At some point not choosing to stand on God's side is choosing to stand in the way of God's purposes.

Day 166

There is news to report. The highest court is now in session and is issuing long awaited rulings.

The first order of business is to set the record straight about God.

God exists and is decisively active in history.

Life has a goal.
Life is headed somewhere.

It is not random chaos or an endless cycle of good winning over bad, then bad winning over good again, ad nauseum.

That would be cruel.

The court knows where lies about God and God's creation come from.

Wicked regimes don't have enough police officers and soldiers to force compliance in a large population. They need people to give up and comply in advance, without a struggle.

Those who teach that there is no purpose to existence or any lasting progress toward justice slander God.

The idea is - if creation has no purpose, and that any good work will only be reversed in the next cycle, why bother?

These teachers find sponsors in the rich and powerful who want to make sure their unjust regimes will not be overthrown.

Day 167

Good and bad are not equally matched.

Good is stronger than bad but must prove itself so.

If good is not stronger than bad it is not good.

It is precisely the centuries long, multi-generational struggle against bad that calls out the full strength of God's goodness in us, which otherwise lies dormant.

Strength reveals itself in the ability to discern, to choose, and to commit our very lives to what God wants most.

Strength shows itself in the skill to effectively pass God's ethic along to our offspring.

Day 168

In God's distribution system if we need a capacity and use it - we get more of it. If we don't use a capacity we lose it over time. Our bodies work that way, so do our minds.

We will need the full power of choice and persistence to overcome the lies that ruin the earth.

God does not meet us with new strength before we choose, or when we avoid choosing, or when we intellectualize or rant about how hard the choice is.

God meets us in the hard choices, when we engage the complexities of our real situation, for as long as it takes to find our way through.

The long struggle screens out the posers.

Day 169

What is best is what supports God's goal for life on earth.

We don't' know the goal and our own goals are no substitute for it.

Only the Creator knows the goal.

But we do know by long direct experience that God is neither cruel nor stupid, but rather good and wise. From what we have helped with so far we know the goal will involve an ever-higher complexity: astonishing diversity that works together as a whole in ever-new combinations.

The richness we see in nature starts to unfold in ourselves. Chaos gives way to fluid, emerging order, calmness replaces anxiety. High diversity and high organization mark our thoughts, our personal lives, and our work.

Day 170

God is the uncreated Creator. God existed before creation and will exist after it is gone. Yet when we look we find God's unlimited intelligence embedded in creation at every level.

Those who do see the vast intelligence at work in creation can become more wise and helpful. It is wisdom to grasp that we are created. We did not create ourselves. We are creative but are not The Creator. We create by using things that already existed. God alone creates out of nothing.

The mark of how much intelligence someone has is how quickly they recognize a greater intelligence and how much they appreciate it.
Those who do not see a vast intelligence at work in creation are not very intelligent and it is foolish to trust or follow them anywhere.

Day 171

Those who deny God usually want to replace God with themselves or their group as the supreme authority.

We do not try to replace God or merge with God because as creatures we are not equal to God.

People who think they have merged with God inevitably think whatever they desire strongly is what God wants, so it is OK to do anything to get what they want, even if that means hurting others.

We reject the dangerous idea of becoming one with God because we know we don't know everything. We can only grasp the interests of a small slice of life for a small slice of time.

No matter how educated we are we can't know what is best for all of creation for all time. We can't be all places at once to see how things are going and make timely adjustments.

Even the sun is only so big and will last only so long. We also exist within set limits. We can't change some things. Only God can make anything happen anywhere at any time.

God alone is limitless.
That is the glory of God.

God alone can bring it all to completion no matter what stands in the way.

There is great comfort in knowing it is God we are helping, that God is ultimately responsible for seeing the work through, and that we only need to do our part.

Day 172

Since we can't know what is best we can't effectively direct our amazing God-given capacities. The first capacity we must learn to direct is our attention because attention directs all our other capacities.

We can only re-learn how to manage our attention in silence and solitude, by looking away from all rivals for our attention.

Our actions, even our most well-intentioned ones, often have unintended consequences.

In trying to help we often make things worse.

The road to hell is indeed paved with good intentions and travelled confidently by those who try to play God.

To function properly we learnt to establish a stable ethical signal directly from God to regulate our behaviors.

Our own actions and those of others can disrupt God's signal into our minds. Mass culture and mass media create so much noise the signal gets drowned out.

We turn away from all media and learn the richness of silence.

We can't re-establish a stable two-way signal on our own.

We must constantly ask God to do that work in us, with our active participation, alone in silence, with the models of nature close at hand.

Day 173

At first getting that signal going at all is hard. It is like digging a tunnel through a mountain of solid rock. But we find the effort is mutual. God is digging from the other side. We are digging through and discarding cunning nonsense from our culture, built up over thousands of years.

We reach for God. We call out for help.

"God, please help me. I pray for grace and wisdom. Help me see, feel, hear, know, understand, respond, become, and embody what is useful to you and your purposes."

God reaches through the noise of the culture and meets us. Often using nature, God teaches us a better normal and pull us out of the culture.

In contact with creation, we sense the calm presence of an Infinite Mind. We feel God's touch.

The channel opens, light enters along with fresh air. The signal begins flowing back and forth. We ask questions and get surprisingly simple answers, sometimes while we are asking, sometimes within 24 hours, usually within a week.

What we need to do next may not be easy, but it is doable. As we change our behavior God's happiness moves along with that signal just as music travels to us on sound wave. We hear the music of creation, mingled with gentle, quiet, kind words.

God never screams at us. If you hear screaming inside or outside your head it is not from God.

Day 174

There is news to report.

The court's second order of business is to set the record straight about God's competence as Creator.

Pay close attention to nature's design and you will see evidence of suffering, desire, and attachment.

No creature in nature suffers to pay for something it did in a past life. That is not why creatures suffer.

God gave us the capacity to suffer, to desire and to make attachments. That is no mistake.

God is not incompetent or cruel.

Day 175

God gave us the capacity to suffer for a reason.

Suffering is the path we take to become useful to God and helpful to life on earth, as it opens our eyes and hearts to the suffering around us.

God gave us the capacity to feel powerful desire for a reason. It was no mistake. Desire is what moves us to overcome inertia and act, even if it is costly or involves risk.

Being helpful, confronting the causes of unjust suffering on earth, will sometimes require action that is costly and risky.

Day 176

God gave us the capacity to form deep and lasting attachments. We use this capacity to form a trusting relationship with God. We use this capacity to form groups that define our identity. We use this capacity to combine forces to solve problems none of us can solve alone.

Attachment lies at the heart of all our most powerful creative capacities.

Life itself passes into the future through parenting, which is a lifetime exercise in mutual attachment.

Severed from the capacity to form attachments, we cannot parent or serve the purposes of justice. God would never ask you to sever such a vital capacity.

Who would want you to give up the wonderful capacity to form attachments?

A wicked ruling regime that wants to preserve their privileges and power.

Rulers throughout history hire clever thinkers to create

religions that are useful to them. The point is to stop the masses from joining together, rising up and revolting against exploitation and forced stupidity.

Cunning religions exist to prevent needed change from happening. They always sever direct personal contact with God.

We attach deeply to God, to nature and to those entrusted to our care.

We attach loosely to everything else.

Day 177

The clever thinkers who sold their services to the powerful are right about one thing. If blocked from constant contact with God, suffering, desire, and attachment lead nowhere and combine to make us miserable.

Guided by God, suffering, desire, and attachment combine to make us uniquely helpful among all the creatures on earth.

The personal bliss that may come from pushing away suffering, desire and attachment is not worth the loss of our greatest capacity as a species – creative and courageous collaboration.

God has plans for those capacities but first moves through our souls to re-worked and re-directed them. We learn to cultivate and harness the capacities God put in us for God's purposes, not to remove them.

Day 178

Once we have a stable daily connection to receive God's quiet ethical guidance, our ability to suffer, to desire and to form attachments combine in ever new ways to solve ever new problems.

It is the way of life.

These very capacities, which bedeviled us when we thought we knew best, now assist the efforts of The One who does know what is best on earth and for earth's future.

Day 179

Bring your suffering, desires, and attachments to God. Having them is not bad. Having them does not make you bad. But mismanaging them is bad for you and the lives around you.

You can't manage them alone because they are bigger than you.

Once entrusted to God, over time, these powerful internal forces will bring goodness into your life and the lives of others.

Suffering teaches empathy, bringing compassion and mercy.

Mercy provides a margin of error when someone is struggling to unlearn something that doesn't work and learn what does work.

Mercy is a lubricant that lowers the friction between people who are struggling together to solve a problem larger than any of them.

Guided by God, desire finally learns what really

satisfies, bringing contentment and patience.

Patience is what allows us to work through many possible combinations until something new emerges that works better than what was there before.

Attachment learns to grip nothing more tightly than it deserves, bringing freedom, flexibility, and open-handed generosity.

Combine compassion, mercy, contentment, patience, freedom, flexibility, and generosity, and you have a very different happiness living among a very different people.

You have God's happiness.

Day 180

Unlike the universe, God did not have a beginning and will never cease to exist.

God made the universe, but God is not the universe. We don't address the universe as God any more than we would talk to a book as if it were its author.

We hold tightly to God, not to the universe or anything in it. Everything in the universe is changing and will someday cease to exist. We hold all created things loosely, knowing God only entrusted them to us for a time to serve God's purposes.

We don't get involved in the fads and drama that will be forgotten in a year.

Day 181

God also made us with the ability to feel remorse. It is an essential part of being useful.

When we cross a line into the life of another creature an alarm goes off designed to help regulate our behavior. When we acknowledge the alarm and promptly correct our behavior, we build a functioning social control system.

Anything that breaks down this control system is not from God.

No one else's virtuous deeds or sacrifice takes away your guilt. Taking guilt away makes it more likely you will do harm again because you think adverse consequences won't fall on you, which is a lie.

Day 182

Guilt that is yours, not guilt put on you by someone else, prompts you to replace old harmful social behaviors with new helpful ones.

God does not run a credit and debit system. God does not transfer someone else's sacrifice to our account to offset our selfish choices.

God is not a bookkeeper. God does not run a bank in which you can borrow someone else's goodness from long ago.

We are part of nature.

God already has a natural way to deal with wrongdoing: bad consequences + unlearning + relearning = new and better consequences.

All other creatures eventually replace dysfunctional actions that imperil their future with functional actions that secure their future.

We learn from the consequences that fall on ourselves and others what is dysfunctional and harmful.

We stop doing what is dysfunctional no matter how popular or traditional it is.

We seek God's guidance and begin again.

We pay attention to our conscience, to God's quiet, gentle guidance and to the models we find in nature. We research to find out what has failed and what has worked well when others have tried it in the past.

We learn what is functional and helpful and then practice and refine it until we are reliably helpful.

Day 183

God gave each creature a body and local resources to sustain that body through its own efforts.

Like any other creature we must effectively protect our physical safety and secure enough material resources to support ourselves and those we love. We don't expect anyone else to do that for us. Strong goodness is self-reliant.

Freedom requires self-reliance.

We have internal signals that tell us when we need sleep and when we have gotten enough sleep, when we need food and when we have had enough food.

God's internal ethical signal will tell us when we have secured enough resources to take care of ourselves and those entrusted to us.

Day 184

Next we turn our attention to creating mutual beneficial relationships with others that help them become self-reliant.

As agents of God's happiness, we object when any individual, group or institution is harming the body of another creature or stealing the resources God gave another creature for its support.

We oppose actions that disrupt the self-reliance of others because they are crimes.

We do not treat disagreement as a crime because it is not.

We do not treat being different as a crime because it is not.

Day 185

Criminals use force and fraud.

Criminals in dark alleys injure the bodies or property of others or threaten to do so.

Criminals in glimmering towers conjure up mesmerizing illusions to send people chasing a happiness that doesn't exist and cannot satisfy.

Both kinds of criminals do this to steal the resources God put in people's hands to support themselves.

If you use force, fraud, or flattery to get what you want, then you are far from God.

If you use persuasion and integrity to direct others to what God wants, then you walk with God.

Day 186

We are different. To influence the values and behaviors of others we use observable facts, reason, and reliable helpfulness.

Our behaviors are puzzling to others.
They spend their days oscillating between fear and greed.

We don't. They want to know why.
Something else calms our minds and motivates our actions. They notice we don't use force or fraud. They want to know why.

They open a case in the court of their imagination.

We are the curious case of the godly soul.

Day 187

The ability to ask WHY is a divine gift to humanity. It always leads us to the discovery of causes that are not immediately apparent but are very real. It is the seed of change.

Under the force of the WHY question some will suspect we behave differently because we have something going on inside that they lack. That stubborn fact is something they can't forget even if they want to. It will bother them. They know they are missing out on something.

The frustrating fact of God's existence and power is now in the mix.

God, The Uncaused Cause – is the cause of our unusual behavior, an invisible force that pulls us out of our prisons.

Day 188

No creature in nature does what is right to earn access to a better place after death where it will live in ease forever.

No creature does the right thing because it is afraid of going to a terrible place after death filled with horrible suffering. In nature, creatures do the right thing because they were made to do so.

If other creatures don't need to be bribed or threatened to do the right thing, neither do we.

God designed us with the capacity to comprehend and happily do the right thing.

When God's directional signal is restored, that is what we start to do.

Loving loyalty to God is as natural to us as seeking the sun is to a tree.

Day 189

Don't seek God's forgiveness. If you feel God's anger at your behavior - good! It means you have a functional conscience. That is God cutting through the mountain of the culture's nonsense, reaching for you.

Instead, start digging from your side of the mountain. Approach God with a contrite heart. Ask to be taught and corrected until you no longer need to be forgiven as often.

Don't ask others to forgive you.
Instead, acknowledge the harm you have caused and express your remorse for doing do. Compensate them for any loss you have caused.

Then learn from God how to behave better until it is second nature.

Day 190

Once you have established a new, sustained track record of creating mutual-benefit relationships others will start to forget their anger.

Forgetting is far better than forgiving because it saves energy that we can put to better use elsewhere.

That is all forgiveness is – ceasing to be angry. We can't ask for it or demand it. We can only deserve it by starting over and building a new track record, which is all God ever wanted anyway.

You will feel God's anger reverse into approval. God's opposition to your efforts will reverse into opportunities to serve because you can now be trusted to protect and care for other creatures so that they can fulfill their place in God's design for life.

Day 191

God gave us the capacity to be very unhappy. Like physical pain, unhappiness registers that something is wrong. Usually, it is a combination of things we are doing and things others are doing to us.

We cause some of our own unhappiness, but not all of it. Our unhappiness often registers something about our social environment.

Loneliness is not the lack of people to interact with. It is about the quality of the people we have around us. We sense it is very unlikely we will be able to form mutually beneficial relationships with them. They are just too selfish. We are not imagining it. The absence of truly helpful people is real, and it causes anxiety, anger, depression, and physical symptoms. It disturbs our sleep.

Day 192

God created us as a social species. We have some of our greatest joy acting creatively in concert with others. We have some of our greatest sorrow when we can't do that. Much of our unhappiness is the lack of God's happiness on Earth.

If we don't feel a problem personally we don't take it seriously enough to solve it. What if God also takes that same problem personally and seriously? To be close to God and helpful to God we must also.

God's happiness does not come from taking nothing seriously, trying to be a carefree, pleasure-soaked kid forever.

God's happiness catches up to us when we accept our responsibilities as competent adults.

Day 193

We have a calling once we take something seriously and personally that God also takes seriously and personally. God takes it seriously because it impacts more than just our personal lives. Our calling usually comes into our lives in a package of painful struggle, as we personally experience the loss or absence of something that is necessary for any life to flourish.

We start to see how that loss or absence is strangling life's full potential elsewhere in other lives. We finally see what God has seen all along.

As we start to see the world through God's eyes, others start to sense God's presence in our eyes.

Day 194

By the age of thirty who has not experienced an undeserved loss or the continuing absence of something vital?

It is common for the calling experience to happen long before that, in adolescence. Our minds are so fluid at that age that it is an immense advantage to start then.

We learn how to work for God by taking our own case of injustice to the Highest Court and watching what happens.

No work of fiction can compare with what starts to unfold from there.

Day 195

God fits us to address our calling with unique inborn abilities honed by unique formative experiences. God tunes our hearts and minds to sense and follow the ethical signal. God then creates unique openings to move into.

As a result, our lives don't turn into a copy of other people's lives, manufactured in mass to do nothing more than produce, and consume, gloat, and complain.

Instead, somehow we end up being just the right person, at just the right place, at just the right time place to meet a need that has always been there. In our later years we know a sense of purpose and completeness that is unavailable to those who live apart from God.

Day 196

There are a few simple ways to document our progress toward finding our calling: one is our attitude toward chores. Especially unscheduled ones.

Life requires constant upkeep. Upkeep is the reversing of disorder as soon as it shows up.
Upkeep requires chores. When we can do our chores well, in a timely manner, happily, and look for lessons from God in them, we are moving along nicely. It means we think of ourselves as part of a living community.

We know we receive benefits from our community. It feels natural and honorable to help take care of what takes care of us.

Expecting a child to do chores affirms the child's sense of belonging and competence.

Day 197

Another way to document progress is spontaneous affection. As we go about our daily affairs we encounter lives that are different than our own, human, and non-human.

If we feel a growing attachment to some of them, if we look forward to interacting with them, if we enjoy their company and seek ways to create enjoyment for them, we are moving along nicely.

Where there is affection there will be spontaneous laughter, delighting in the unplanned moment, without cruelty.

Day 198

Spontaneous affection forms a mutually protective bond of attachment.

Without even planning to we find ourselves growing, sharing, and savoring the common stock of God's happiness.

God is present among us.

God has a marvelous sense of humor. Hilarious things happen you just had to be there to fully appreciate. You laugh together until you cry.

These shared moments move us from always saying "I, me, mine" to saying "we, us, ours."

We no longer feel so alone.

Day 199

Before establishing daily contact with God's ethical signal, when other creatures were out of sight - they were out of mind. Now the lives we feel attached to are always on our minds. Their well-being and happiness are inseparable from our own. If they hurt, we hurt. If they thrive, we celebrate without envy. We feel our living connection to other lives and all of nature.

Anxiety, anger, and depression of loneliness starts to ease among us because we sense it is likely we will be able to create and sustain mutually beneficial relationships.

We are becoming a loving, attentive, competent, and inventive people. We are taking on the attributes of The One we admire most.

Day 200

We are on holy ground anywhere people start to happily help each other, spontaneously and consistently. Where there is voluntary helpful cooperation without paying a professional to organize it all, God is pleased. That place stands apart from other places.

Though simple, the act of happily helping each other provides something no amount of luxury can – a solid social base made up of goodwill and loyalty.

Goodwill is our commitment to be there for each other in a time of need and to celebrate each other's successes. Loyalty is our commitment to protect each other's reputation and interests when the other is absent and cannot do it for themselves.

It is the beginning of a new society, one fit for a long and helpful tenure on earth.

Day 201

The happiness we feel now is as great as the unhappiness we felt when we started, when we were far from such a helpful place.

We marvel at the reversal God has brought about. We never could have planned it. It was completely dependent on unforeseen events God used to open situations and then guided us to enter and improve.

It happened in a place we never would have chosen.

We are so happy that we sought and then followed God's corrective, creative signal.

Day 202

The voice inside that shouts "More for me - faster!
Everything I can imagine - for me!" is not a calling. It is
a form of moral brain cancer.

It will not stop until it has eaten your soul alive and
ruined your relationships and reputation.

 That is not the voice of God.

"You can channel God's power to get all those things."
Beware of such teachings.
Magic is *reality-as-I wish-it-to-be* rather than reality as it is,
known by direct contact and experience.

As a rule of thumb, any notion that does nothing to
strengthen your desire for justice on earth is not from
God and is best to discard.

Day 203

Magic is the systematic practice of delusion.

Magic is not being with God in contact with reality, but rather willfully fleeing God and contact with reality.

It is attempting to use God's power to force reality to match our envious wishes, wishes we often got from advertising or fawning stories about celebrities.

Magical thinking completely blocks God's ethical signal because it has no ethical content at all.

There is no "we" in magic.
It is all about "me."

Day 204

Any notion that The Creator is a thing, an inanimate, mindless force we can harness to turn our fantasies into reality is insulting to God. It sets up a rival to God in our hearts.

Magic nurtures insatiable desires and turns them into our new god, our source of direction. Magic will never direct us away from harming or neglecting those who get in the way of our "dreams," but instead will justify any harm we cause as unfortunate but necessary to "follow our bliss."

Magical thinking is a kind of sleepwalking. It is dangerous to us and those around us.

Magical thinking puts individuals, groups, even entire civilizations on a path to ruin.

Day 205

We don't need wishes and dreams to guide our choices because we have a growing sense of reality and our duty to life itself. The unfolding reality God has in store for us to discover and cultivate is better than any human wish or dream.

In addition, whereas the wishes and dreams of one human or human group quickly conflicts with the wishes and dreams of another, God's guidance leads out of and away from unnecessary destructive conflict.

We know we are moving toward God, toward our calling when we start to feel a strange new sensation: contentment.

Once I have sense of what God called me to do I can see how God is using my situation to prepare me to do it.

God does not promise me tomorrow, and I can't do anything about yesterday, so if I have enough to do something to advance God's purposes on earth *today*, I am content. The madness of insatiable desire starts to fade away.

Day 206

When learning to speak a new language in a place where people speak it, there comes a day when what was once just noise suddenly comes together and carries meaning.

You find yourself dreaming and thinking in that new language rather than constantly translating between your first and second language.

In the same way there comes a day when we can spot the amount that is enough to do our duty today. It was always there but we did not see it. Now we do. We seek no more.

We learn over time that God provides for us and always will. We rarely know ahead of time how it will happen, but we know with increasing certainty that it will. This assurance frees up attention to go toward the needs of the lives around us.

 Life begins to unfold around us in ways we never could have imagined.

Day 207

Species go extinct that do not evolve when their environment changes. They are replaced by new species whose behaviors allow them to thrive in their new environment.

Humans are not exempt from this rule. We didn't write it, and we can't change it, we can only prove it to be true.

Once we re-establish constant contact with God and gain a sense of what we have been uniquely entrusted to cultivate, we start evolving again as an individual, a group, and a species.

We regain the lost capacities of the soul and develop new ones we can't even imagine today that will fit us for challenges we also can't imagine today.

Day 208

No government, no corporation, no charity, can provide for and protect us the way God can because they can't foresee the future.

We don't look to those sources for anything more than temporary solutions. We know, lacking God's design wisdom, their solutions degrade and eventually become problems.

Instead, in troubling times we fall silent, look to God, and follow the instructions we receive.
That distinctive behavior sets us apart and makes us uniquely useful.

To be holy is to be set apart for specialized use.
To be saved is to be preserved in safety for later use.

Day 209

Sometimes we get stuck and need a repair shop for our minds. It is best to spend as little time in these places as possible, though sometimes it is necessary.

The point of a repair shop is to get us back on the road as soon, as safely and as cheaply as possible, not to hold us there for years, taking apart even more systems.

Since so much of our happiness is about relationships, a repair expert who has no good relationships is not a resource to help you with your unhappiness.

It doesn't matter what document is hanging on the wall. What matters is how they treat others in their own lives.

Day 210

If you can't verify first-hand the quality of a repair expert's primary relationships, don't seek their help for too long. Don't believe everything you hear. As soon as you have learned how to use some solid reality-testing and problem-solving tools on your own, move on.

If the expert does not direct you back to God you are not being helped. If the expert directs you toward anything but nature as the standard of good design, you are being harmed. If the expert teaches you to numb your conscience so you can feel no discomfort while being more selfish, you are being harmed. If any expert mocks your love for God or tries to replace God in your life it is time to leave and to warn those you love to stay away from the expert.

In the eyes of others, what we don't do defines us as much or more than what we do.

Others notice who we don't associate ourselves with, what we don't endorse with our attention, involvement, and money. Just by not participating, without a word, we are saying a lot.

Day 211

It is not mental health to become happily well-adjusted to a world-system God did not build and will never support. It is madness.

We may gain some temporary relief, but we add nothing to the stock of happiness on earth.

If there is no study of nature and history, no development of empathy or a concern for justice, you are being harmed.

If there is talk of getting more power, directing energy, channeling, and manifesting someone is teaching magic. The energy behind magic is always envy and resentment.

Envy and resentment poison the soul.

Day 212

In God's repair shop we experience something better than adjusting better so we can succeed in a selfish society. Instead, we learn to adjust to earth. As a result, we experience healing that goes way beyond just getting back to doing what the culture says is valuable.

We also experience something better than redemption. Redemption is about repaying a creditor. God is not a creditor and we are not debtors. Nobody likes creditors and nobody likes being in debt.

Rather than adjustment or redemption, we experience repatriation. God calls to go home and fits for the journey and the work that will commence when we get there.

Going home is a life adventure. We don't live under the burden of guilt or the fear of missing out. We live within the creative tension of adventure that pull us irresistibly toward the horizon of the new.

We live within a migratory, moving community of curiosity, learning discovery, creativity, eager participation, and cooperation.

We find along the way, to our delight, that our different life callings need each other to find completion. Together we optimize any set of circumstances we find, constructing larger, healthier, more diverse living systems motivated by mutual desire to contribute.

Day 213

God made us a free people. We don't use our freedom
to do whatever we want. We use our freedom to
become what God calls us to become because we know
that is the only thing that will make us happy.

God freely give us our lives. God gives each of us a
unique adventure to discover over time how to spend
our lives in a way that will further God's purposes on
earth.

If we reject God's calling embedded in our souls and
spend our lives chasing what the culture tells us will
make us happy we will find ourselves lost in a maze of
contradictions. Nothing turns out the way it was
supposed to.

We can find ourselves again.

We go to God and put at God's disposal what God
freely gave us – our time, attention, loyalty, our ethical
choices, our use of the resources temporarily available
to us. We integrate our lives again into the living system
God created. We replace each lie we once believed
with a truth about how life does things. We replace
each harmful behavior with a helpful one.

Day 214

There are many steps in the process of repatriation and there are no short cuts, so it takes time. Devine repatriation is not an event, a ceremony, or a ritual.

Repatriation requires a long, costly process of reconstruction. We must be re-formatted for the journey. We must learn to repair the broken trust we cause when we harm others because in our new home we will live far more by cooperation than competition.

Repatriation work is possible, and so worth it. Doing the work to start the journey home is the best repair process to use when we get stuck because it restores the only thing that can repair everything else – our sense of empathy and justice.

On the other end of the repatriation process lies God's full happiness. Along the way the old, empty happiness diminishes and God's happiness grows fuller.

The process brings us home to earth and teaches us the laws of life anew.

Day 215

We are not in control of the process of repatriation. Unlike the electricity we access with a wall outlet, mortals don't tap, control, and use The Eternal's power for their petty purposes.

That notion is exactly backwards.

We don't seek to control God.

We learn to finally submit our desires and abilities to God's control.

Only then do we know peace and find we can do practical things to bring peace into the world.

Day 216

God's control does not eliminate our freedom and creativity, it makes the most of our freedom and creativity when God needs them most. And that day will surely come.

In God's repair shop, through the lengthy process of getting ready to go home, we gain the clarity, courage, and competence to be calm and decisive under pressure.

Events are coming that will require these virtues. We won't freeze and run away when trouble comes. We will protect the innocent.

In those moments we will be glad we went through the process of repatriation because it is what produces strong goodness. In crisis, nothing less will do.

Day 217

We did not put ourselves together, so we don't know how to take ourselves apart and put ourselves back together in a new and better way. We don't know what to remove that won't fit as part of earth. We don't know what needs to be built into our lives that we will need to be part of earth.

No human advisor is your Creator. Trusting another human to deconstruct you and your problems will leave you deconstructed for sure. But there is no way another human can put you back together to fit the situation you were born to fit into and optimize, since it does not yet exist.

The One we are dependent upon to remake us is Our Maker. That voluntary dependency is not weak.

It is the greatest power we have.

Day 218

We resist ongoing dependency on anyone or anything else but God, including substances. It is a shortcut to nowhere.

We voluntarily develop a deep dependency upon the One who knows us best and knows what is best for earth.

We can do that because we trust most the One we love most.

Realistically, at any moment we could lose any form of human support upon which we might depend. It is not possible to lose God.

We already know how to pull ourselves together. We do it anytime we want something badly. We are better at this than we realize.

After we have learned to use a few useful tools in the repair shop, we can pull yourselves together our own way to meet God's standards.

Day 219

God's happiness is not what we feel when we win over others, it is what we feel when we benefit others. Life contains games but God did not design life as a game. God designed life as a community.

Other lives are not our rivals or opponents. They are neighbors and potential partners in constructing a larger, richer, more diverse, more resilient environment all of us can draw upon through thick and thin.

Time spent focusing on how to get what we want at the expense of others is time spent disconnected from God's guiding signal. The voice we hear that tells us to win at all costs is the voice of madness. It will invariably tell us it is OK to harm the innocent who get in our way.

There is a natural, limited time and place for playing games in God's design. More about that later.

Day 220

To love winning for the sake of winning means to love causing loss for others. To play games we enter a contrived situation with made up rules that exist nowhere in nature. We learn to get better and better at doing something that God doesn't need done in the first place.

We will inevitably apply those competitive lessons to those we live with, treating them as rivals for no other reason than that they have legitimate support needs. The outcome is simply to strangle God's happiness in the very place we go to recover.

God calls and equips us to struggle for the sake of justice and it is no game. God does not teach us gaming skills. God is not the Gamer; God is the Creator. God teaches us creativity skills.

Day 221

God does not exist to help us win our contrived games. God does not take sides in our contrived games. God is not our secret weapon or power move.

Human culture disconnected from God and obsessed with surpluses, loves to create games and gamers, winners, and losers. It is what causes most of the pointless suffering on earth.

Focusing on winning as the goal of life will block and then shut off God's directing signal.
The only thing powerful enough to open the channel again is unforeseen loss.

If we build an identity on causing loss to others only catastrophic loss can get our attention and show us what we have been doing to others.

Day 222

Real knowledge shows itself in superior results. When I see results beyond what I can do I know there is knowledge beyond what I have.

Creation is one vast demonstration of an intelligence beyond what humans can do.

The mark of intelligence is the ability to recognize and defer to an intelligence greater than our own.

God's happiness never catches up to us when we think we know more than God, or better than God.

God's happiness starts to catch up to us when we acknowledge and admire the genius of creation as beyond anything humans have ever done or will ever do.

Day 223

We see the infinite intelligence embedded in creation and sense how much greater it is than our own, which is amazing, but finite. We admire what we see and become receptive.

We start to learn that our finite minds can only operate at their best when guided by an infinite mind. We unlearn what we must to make space for what we will learn.

We don't make the rules, we learn the rules that already govern life. We unlearn rules that don't work.

God brings us to a reliable state of competence like any other mature creature in nature. With us in the mix things stop getting worse and start getting better.

Day 224

We don't take the word of people who claim to know best just because they have an impressive degree and work for a famous institution.

We require first-hand evidence of good relationships and outcomes. Marketing and hearsay will not do.

We require way more than one example. The results must be directly accessible and replicable.

We must see a long pattern of superior results in an authority's own life, in their own organization and from their applied work.

We require working models, not theories or catchy quotes. We learn poetry is no substitute for precise competence.

Day 225

We don't chase intellectual fads. We don't look for magic bullets, or magic of any kind. We don't seek simplistic, easy solutions to complex problems.

If there is evidence of better outcomes we trust, approach, and start learning. If the evidence is not we move on and keep looking for something better.

Fake experts will be outraged. They expect blind trust, adoration, prompt payment and obedience. That reaction is the sign they are fakes.

True experts' welcome challenges from anyone with a legitimate concern, the more the better. True experts know how essential other minds' observations are to make something more useful or make a system less wasteful.

Day 226

A true expert is happy when you ask to see the evidence for yourself.

A true expert's information is both reliable and accurate. Each new insight does not vary wildly from or contradict the last one. Each new insight represents the described phenomenon without error, omission, or distortion. With each conversation a clearer, more complete picture emerges, one you can safely use to make decisions.

Openness to respectful challenge is the sign we have met someone who honors the genius God embedded in creation. Clear, factual, logical answers given in normal, accessible language is evidence the expert wants you to see for yourself and grasp the information so you can make sound decisions without them around.

It is rare for anyone to ask to see the information the true expert has put decades into collecting. You have become in good company. Your genuine interest relieves some of their loneliness.

Day 227

God's happiness comes from trusting God's way of doing things. Healthy trust requires reason. It does not require ignoring reason or believing fantastic and illogical stories.

Learned confidence starts by carefully observing something that is happening right now, right here. God has already provided the curriculum we need in nature. We can see for ourselves that life is doing wonderful things in wonderful ways.

After observation we start to wonder – how did that come to be and how does it work? What will happen next? We use logic, we gather more facts to work out a cause-and-effect sequence that makes sense and can be tested. The more we can prove, the more respect we feel for the vast intelligence of The Creator.

Day 228

God gave us eyes, ears, a conscience, and the ability the reason. If things don't add up, we don't trust. We don't learn from those we don't trust.

We should withhold our trust when bad things are happening that shouldn't happen according to the current theory or ancient tradition.

We should withhold our trust when good things aren't happening that should be happening by now, according to the current theory or ancient tradition.

Things never add up when others lead toward a mirage using clever propaganda. When we arrive, there is nothing there.

Day 229

When a whole combination of claims roll into a narrative that doesn't add up others have led us right into quicksand.

It may be a large, elaborate, integrated structure that goes on and on, but it is deadly.

The harder we struggle to try to support the current theory or ancient fable the more ludicrous our explanations become, the weirder the language we must use.

To associate ludicrous explanations with God is to slander God.

God is not ludicrous.

Day 230

There is news to report. Court is still in session and wants to set the record straight.

God is just and would never require harming the innocent, the neighbor, the stranger. God doesn't set peaceful neighbors against each other.

To secure protection and blessing God will never ask a people to commit what would otherwise be genocide were it not done in God's name.

Lies about how God does things lead to atrocities. Lies only move in one direction – more crazy and more violent.

Just because a civilization now only vents its madness on other species does not make it more enlightened than ones that once tried to wipe out an entire minority group.

Day 231

The greatest barrier to God's happiness is nonsense that never made sense in the first place. Nonsense is usually an ancient lie or current fad, or some new combination of the two. Current fads are very often just updated versions of ancient lies.

If we were honest with ourselves, we would admit it never made sense in the first place. Upon hearing ancient fables kids roll their eyes and groan. They are often more honest than adults and don't want their own futures saddled with nonsense. Good for them!

We find ourselves entangled in nonsense when we trust others to do for us what we can only do for ourselves.

In contrast, when we do our own thinking and use observation, reason, and experiments, guided by God, we untangle ourselves from nonsense.

Finally, life starts to make sense.

Day 232

Life makes sense. There is reason in what is real and always has been. We sense deeply embedded reason when we see how the parts of something natural combine into a working whole.

Life makes sense when God directs our actions using observation, reasoning, and testing, following the examples in nature and history.

Life makes sense when we follow our conscience and act out of empathy, when we are around people who say what they mean and mean what they say, when we make and keep agreements, follow up on conversations and follow through on what we promised to do in a timely manner.

The reason this all makes sense is that God made us social species. God's happiness flows into our lives through shared, social experience, not personal comfort, and pleasure.

Day 233

God never asks us to close our eyes, plug our ears, dull our consciences, turn off our brains to follow the crowd, or to just swallow what someone says.

It doesn't matter what costume the person is wearing, how monumental the architecture is, how spectacular the show is, or how big an audience someone has gathered. Nonsense needs a big show to convince quickly but truth doesn't.

Truth convinces slowly because it unfolds slowly and quietly, in small places and intimate experiences.

God's happiness catches up to us to the same degree that we toss out nonsense, verify facts, vindicate truth, and secure justice by the way we treat all the lives around us.

Day 234

No creature can be happy for long in a complex and changing environment if it is not competent. Among social animals it is impossible to be happy for long living among others who are not competent. It can get you killed.

As members of a social species, we must be competent enough at competing to secure a situation in which we can support our continued existence. Then, we must be competent at cooperating enough with others to construct together a larger, richer situation that supports the continued existence of many other and different lives. If we are not competent at all three of these activities and know when to move from one to the next, we are incompetent.

Education does not produce competence. Training produces competence.

Training is composed of study followed immediately by practice. We don't separate study from practice. Study informs practice and practice corrects the gaps in what we study.

In training we break the task down into steps, practice

each step separately and then practice putting the steps together. When it all comes together to produce competence we feel happy.

It is a well-deserved happiness - from God.

Day 235

When a hard-won, newly acquired ability overcomes an obstacle that always stopped us before – we experience the feeling of triumph.

Effective training leads to triumph. Triumph is the feeling of newly earned freedom. We now have more options and the ability to access them. The newness of the experience of triumph makes it different and far greater than just another success like the last one or the feeling of winning at the expense of others.

As God cultivates us into full maturity we get to feel the thrill of triumph when we achieved voluntary cooperation between people who are different from each other. We can then move on to construct something new that takes care of all of us and the earth at the same time and share the feeling of triumph with others – which doubles its enjoyment. We are learning how God does diversity.

Triumph is a feeling we can't get by being flattered or soothed, or by making any purchase, or by watching any performance. Triumph is a more enjoyable sensation than any intoxicating substance.

Day 236

Triumph is a happiness God built into life. It is waiting for those who earn it. It catches up to us and surprises us. Suddenly we feel ourselves surpassing our own internal limits after a long struggle.

It is fair and just. We have earned it through our own efforts. It is God's built-in way of rewarding what is worthy, what is excellent, what is useful.

We can now trust ourselves enough to go places and attempt things we could not have before, while seeking and following God's guidance.

We have won the freedom to act responsibly. That is what real freedom is.

Day 237

Magic promises simple and easy success without the struggle of training. It robs us of the experience of triumph and instead creates a fragile confidence that will shatter the first time it encounters harsh reality.

We don't pursue magical solutions. We pursue mastery and excellence so we can be useful in service of God's priorities on earth. There is toil and struggle, but the experience is not all toil and struggle, not by any means.

Daily, we tap into free energy just as the hawk soars on thermal updrafts, warmed by the sun. God guides us into openings we did not foresee or force in which we can create combinations that were not possible before. We do our part, but we know all along God does the decisive parts and holds the grand strategy.

There is a happiness in excellence that is worth the struggle it demands. Achieving excellence builds sturdy confidence, vindicated the moment we must engage in a harsh reality that was there all along.

God rewards any helpful work done with excellence with something as rare as it is valuable - joy.

Day 238

Daily doses of joy sustain God's happiness. It is the feeling of useful freedom.

Joy is the feeling of fruitfulness, of having a gift that keeps giving more gifts.

The joy of competence combines with a feeling of greater security. Once acquired, no one can take our competence from us, and we can use it to meet our own needs in almost any situation.

We often use pleasure to make up for an absence of real joy in our lives. Once we have tasted well-earned, God-given joy, we don't need as much pleasure as we used to and get more satisfaction out of the simple, inexpensive pleasures of daily life.

Day 239

Freedom is not permission to do anything we want. We are free to choose between options, but we are not free to choose the consequences of our choice. The consequences are bound up in the choice itself. The consequences may not arrive immediately, but they certainly will arrive, often at the worst possible time.

The consequences of our past choices limit or expand the options we can choose from in the future. Freedom is the ability to bring about the most goodness in any situation in which God places us. If our hands are tied, we have no freedom to affect change.

If we give up freedom to have security, it is a bad bargain. We end up with neither freedom nor security.

The safest place on earth is alongside God. In fact, it is the only safe place to be.

Day 240

Soul is the mind's capacity to feel sympathy with another mind. A soulless person is someone you can't connect with, can't trust, can't rely upon for help in time of need.

Soulless people form attachments to soulless things, not to living creatures. A soulless person will try to control and possess other living things, but it is a one-way relationship. The soulless person takes at the expense of the other and gives nothing back.

A soulless person feels dead inside.
A soulful person feels alive inside.

Animals don't like soulless people and soulless people don't like animals. Animals love most enthusiastically those with the most soul, as do children. The sick, disabled, and aged sense they are seen and safe around those with a skilled, working soul.

Day 241

What we give attention to grows, what we ignore shrinks. The soul's sympathy is a pathway, a conduit. If we ignore the pathway, it narrows.

If we attend to substitutes for God's happiness, they swell in the narrowing conduit. At some point we find the pathway blocked. Nothing can get through from either side. The result is we can't talk to God and God can't talk to us. We can't learn from nature and nature can't teach us anything. We can't listen to others, and they grow tired of listening to us brag or complain. No vital information is exchanged.

When an artery or vein is blocked, cells throughout the body are deprived of oxygen and start to die. Three minutes without oxygen can cause irreversible brain damage. At some point the same thing can happen to our souls.

Day 242

One or two choices of selfishness can start the process of soul death.

We pass the damage on to our children as well. They start life thinking it is good and normal to have no soul. When we reject suffering as useless, then do whatever it takes to run away from it, we lose a degree of soul in the process. We start to think only bad, foolish, or weak people suffer.

When desire tries to direct itself it ignores or tramples the needs of others who get in the way. That destroys trust. Others become hardened around us, and we become hardened around them. More soul dies with each encounter as the world we create gets lonelier and meaner.

Once we allow a blockage to form, all sorts of dysfunctions fester behind it.

Day 243

When attachment seeks to possess and control, it turns others into objects. The soul must be shut down before we can treat friends like things and things like friends.

When humans chase something, certain it will make them happy, they must burn up some of their soul to do it. No matter how successful they become, it shows in their faces. They look more annoyed than happy. Their words are cynical and cutting. They have trophies to show off, but no joy.

They have lost the capacity to know intimate contact with God, with nature, or with those they claim to love. They know how to take, consume, coerce, and use, but not how to love.

The loss of soul is devastating, poisoning all other pleasures.

Day 244

Keep your soul healthy no matter what the cost. Keep the pathway of service unblocked and uncluttered.

The kingdom of God and all its fullness enters human affairs through intimate, local, practical, mutually beneficial relationships with all the life God placed within our reach.

There is no other point of entry, there is no other pathway.

Day 245

It takes time, effort and patience until God's happiness makes us helpful, just as it takes time, effort, and patience to learn a new language.

What sustains our motivation during the long reconstruction process?

Learned confidence.

That is all that faith is.

A plant grows toward the sun. It is possible the sun won't show up, but in fact it does, and always has.

The plant uses an enormous amount of energy to produce a flower, and then it waits.

The bee may never come, but the plant produces a flower anyway.

Day 246

There is an invisible order to things that will outlast and upend what is currently visible.

By relying on what is currently invisible, the plant lives both in and beyond the moment at the same time.

If plants only lived in the moment they would not produce flowers.

Plants participate in life on earth by relying on something beyond themselves to create something that will live on after they die.

Plants demonstrate the same faith we learn in time.

There is more wisdom about faith in an old oak tree than in all the seminaries in the world.

Day 247

I sit on a chair without a second thought because I have learned, through repeated experiences, that a chair will support my weight. I learned by touch, by feel, that I can trust the chair.

No one showed me a theory about chairs. It is the way we learn to do anything upon which life depends. It is how we learned to breathe, drink, eat and reproduce.

In the same way, when we call out to God, we learn we will be met, taught, and helped, without being coddled.

We can be confident of a firm support from an invisible source. Air is invisible but supports birds in flight. Just because something is invisible does mean it is not real.

We learn God will not do for us the things we must do for ourselves. God also will never abandon us as we struggle to learn to do what we alone can do as part of earth.

As the years pass we can't remember the specifics, but we remember the sequence of events that happened.

We know that basic sequence of moves that coordinate our actions with God's infinite mind will be there. With confidence we seek God in any decision that affect the lives of others in any situation we face.

We come to rely upon the process of guided problem-solving just as the plant relies on the process of pollination.

We have learned by touch how to join the dance of life.

Day 248

God does not ask us to believe a set of ideas, theories, or fantastic stories we can't verify in our experience. Those aren't chairs we will sit on. They won't support the weight of real-life decisions.

Those aren't lakes one can drink from. They are mirages. Have you ever witnessed someone rise from the dead or a talking animal? Have you ever witnessed a life after this one lived in a place other than earth? Such nonsense is not faith, it is fantasy.

Attaching unverifiable fantasies to the name of God locks out the finest, the most honest, the most keenly observant minds – the very people we most need to solve the biggest problems we face.

Day 249

To teach resurrection, or past and future lives is to say
God made a mistake in giving us all one life that lasts
for a set period of time and then ends for good.

God gives each creature one life. Are we so greedy as to
demand more than other creatures get? There is only so
much space on earth. Only so many resources.
Creatures die to make room for creatures to come.
Death is a necessary part of life.

If we assume there will be other lives we won't seek
God's guidance to make the most of this one. We take
our chances and give ourselves permission to waste this
life in worldly pursuits.

Instead, godly earthlings accept with gratitude their one
and only life and commit to making it a helpful one. A
thriving earth will be our legacy. There is no better
memorial or evidence of a life well lived.

Day 250

There is news to report. The court wants to set another thing straight about God.

God is invisible and inaudible. Eyes and objects to see were created and did not exist at one time. Ears and sounds to hear did not exist at one time. God is the Creator who existed then and will exist after all visible and audible things are gone.

Any attempt to make God visible or audible is a lie.

The Creator will not be reduced to the form of any creation. To represent God in any artistic form is to misrepresent God.

Representations of God always end up serving a human agenda involving power and money.

We seek God as God is - invisible. To be loyal is to defend the reputation and interests of one who is not visibly present now. We do not accept representations of God among us.

We seek intimacy with our invisible Creator. We live daily, directed, helpful lives on earth, loyal to the

Creator. We defend God's interests in what looks like God's absence to those who never seek God.

In return God is loyal to us when we are no longer around. We will be remembered fondly by God for all eternity, long after the universe is gone. That is the only immortality that exists.

There is no greater lasting monument. There is no higher compliment. There is no heaven that offers a better reward for our loyalty.

Day 251

History proves no person, no organization, no empire is so great as to avoid vanishing from the book of life, completely forgotten.

It may take two thousand years, which is no more than a sneeze in the immense journey of life, but there comes a day when the last person to remember an obscure name mentioned once in an old book - dies.

On that day that name, that life and all it did, ceases to exist. It is as if it never lived at all.
The unhelpful spent their lives proudly forgetting God.
The unhelpful will be forgotten by God and everyone else, passing into utter oblivion.

There is no greater condemnation.
It is only fair.

Day 252

God asks us to notice and trust our own direct
experience, nothing more, nothing else. It is how all
other creatures figure things out.

Over time our experience confirms the daily presence,
wisdom, and power of God.
God does intervene at critical moments. Every time it is
in an unforeseen way and at an unforeseen moment.

God will not be limited to any human program
designed to glorify one human group. Contact with
God will not be bottled and sold in convenient
packages at a reasonable price.

 Those who claim otherwise want glory for themselves
that they have not earned. God will set the record
straight and turn their glory to shame.

There is only One who has earned our highest esteem
and trust.

Day 253

We reflect God's glory in our behaviors, but we never try to direct it, bottle it, or sell it in convenient packages.

We don't offer packages of magic. We don't suggest others can skip training and go straight to effectiveness.

We don't lie about God.

We tell the truth: there is nothing convenient about the glory of God. God's presence and rule will not fit nicely into a busy, worldly life.

God's rule in our hearts will be costly, very inconvenient, and controversial.
But if we pay the price, God's purposes take over our lives to make us truly helpful to life on earth.

Day 254

The sun's energy is a free resource for plants. Plants do nothing to earn it and could never repay it, even as they are completely dependent on it. They use some of it for themselves and freely pass the rest of it on in the form of food for other creatures.

We interact with God's guiding wisdom in the same way. It is an unearned gift, so we do not hoard it or claim to have made it. We don't try to control it; we make use of it and pass it on in ways useful to others.

Plants alone are self-feeders. They can turn energy from the nearest star into food. All other creatures feed on something that would not exist without plants.

In nature, food chains emerge. Nothing is wasted. Every resource gets used over and over.

The system is beautiful, functional, and endlessly innovative. God expects anything we do to live up to this standard. Anything we do that does not live up to this standard will not endure.

Day 255

In God's design, each creature must struggle to secure its own place on earth and enough resources it needs to survive, grow, and provide for its offspring. A sufficient amount of competition is the only thing that can ensure each creature is strong, resourceful, and flexible.

Next, each creature must cooperate to create mutually beneficial relationships with other creatures. In long-lived ecosystems each resident creature does something for another what the other can't do for itself. Each creature in turn receives something it can't make for itself.

A sufficient amount of cooperation is the only thing that can construct a system complex enough to overcome large threats facing all the creatures that share a particular space.

Day 256

In God's happiness our role is one similar to the plants. We are self-feeders.

We get a living system going by absorbing daily enough of God's free wisdom to respond ethically to whatever challenges we face.

Emerging from solitude in God's presence we have enough fuel to take care of ourselves, then to cooperate with others, then to foster a social environment in which mutual helpfulness is natural, expected and rewarded.

We learn, when possible, how to nudge others away from unhelpful behaviors and toward an ethic of helpful cooperation.

We remember how kind and patient God was with us and imitate that behavior with others.

Day 257

Our aim is not to be one of God's helpless children forever. We don't seek to be entertained and coddled. We don't want enchanting fables. We don't want to remain innocent, passive, and naïve. We don't expect to take a free ride, contributing no work in return.

Lofty words won't do. They are no substitute for sturdy habits.

Just as the acorn's aim is to become an oak tree, our aim is to be one of God's mature adults, able to perform all the functions life requires of us, no matter what.

As mature adults we would rather know the truth than be naïve. We learn to see right through popular nonsense to what is really going on.

We would rather tell the truth and deal with the consequences than deny the truth to be popular.

We learn to stand alone when necessary.

We would rather be free to serve God and pay the cost

of that freedom, than be taken care of by others at the cost of being a slave to their purposes.

Mature adults are courageous and decisive.

We learn where true courage comes from and what it does. Courage comes from knowing by experience that we are deeply loved and will never be abandoned.

Courage means refusing to support what God would never support because it harms life.

Day 258

Our aim is not to remain sensation-hording adolescents who flee responsibility. That is not the function of adolescence.

The passage from childhood to adulthood is a time of exploration, to map as much of the world around us as we can.

It is also a time of play, which is another form of exploration. Young animals spend a lot of time playing. Play is unplanned learning. It provides the opportunity to practice moves in a relatively safe setting they will use as adults when the stakes are much higher.

Among us adolescence is an apprenticeship in how to be a helpful, competent, cooperative adult.

Day 259

When animals play, they first signal it is play - it is not serious. Dogs do a play bow.

Both participants agree to the terms. They will not cause each other harm, but they will challenge each other's skills. They will alternate between winning and losing. It will be a limited part of the day. It happens during a limited time in their lives.

Animals play games but do not become lifelong gamers, nor do they make life itself into a game, because it is not.

Animals do not turn every creature they meet into an opponent to crush, or a plaything manipulate, then discard.

Neither do we.

Day 260

We make the most of childhood, playing, learning verses, stories and songs that capture God's expectations and wisdom.

We make the most of adolescence, exploring who we are, what we are good at, and what we find most interesting.

We start to sense our calling – how what we find interesting and natural to do well might fit what needs to be done in the world someday.

A calling, the experiences we need to cultivate our ability to fulfill it, and the opportunity to fulfill it, all come from the same source – our Creator. Our Creator can provide anything for anyone anywhere at any time, even when the society one lives in is unjust and won't even try to do so.

Day 261

"God, please make me rich and famous like (celebrity)."

"God, please give that person as my mate."

"God, please give me this job."

Those are "me" prayers. We all start out praying that way. They are noisy and there are a lot of them.

These prayers mostly come from our earliest notions of magic – trying to control, rather than know, God. It is an attempt to make God into a vending machine.

There is little or no love in "me" prayers. Those who become atheists often do so after a "me" prayer goes unanswered. Atheism is just an extended tantrum.

Day 262

"God, I know I get in the way. I don't represent you well. I hurt others. I am so sorry. My heart's desire is that someday you and I will work together effectively. Please change me until we do."

"God, I am troubled by how my relationship with my partner is going. Please guide us until we interact in a way that pleases you."

"God, it breaks my heart how my organization behaves. We can be so mean. What am I supposed to do when I see that?"

Those are "we" prayers. These prayers arise from someplace much deeper inside.

There is love in "we" prayers.

They are very quiet prayers and there are only a few of them.

Day 263

It is during adolescence that we start making promises to God. Some of them are just trying to make deals to get stuff we think will make us happy. We pray a lot of "me" prayers – asking God to give us things or rescue us from bad things.

But there is a small and quiet voice inside that knows better. It comes from loving respect and offers no deals. It prays heart-felt "we" prayers. It tenderly asks that the quality of our relationship with God will become purer, and less self-absorbed.

A small part of us really wants to use our lives to be truly useful to God. It is usually overpowered by another, selfish voice, but it is there. It is a start. It is the voice of conscience. It knows God deserves no less.

It is the part of us that wants to know God the way God wants to be known.

Years later we realize God remembered and answered all our "we" prayers and few if any of our "me" prayers.

We are glad it worked out that way.

Day 264

"Me" prayers are about the contents of our experience. It is all the things we want to experience or stop experiencing.

"We" prayers are about the structure of our souls. It is how we process any experience we have.

Think about a pear-shaped glass bowl. No matter what contents are placed in it they end up taking on the shape of a pear. Change to a tall cylindrical glass bowl and the same contents will take on a cylindrical shape.

Profound change is not a change in *what* we experience, it is a change in *how* we experience everything.

Day 265

If I respond to frustration, setback or loss the same way with new life contents as I did with the previous life contents I have not changed.

There is no evidence of divine creative power in my life.

On the other hand, if sometime later I spontaneously respond differently to frustration, set-back and loss when no one is watching, something profound has happened.

One of those rare, quiet "we" prayers has been answered. The change will not go unnoticed.

People who know us well will ask the "why" question.

It is a start.

Day 266

Structural change is what God does with our capacity to suffer, desire, and attach. It alters what we do with our time and attention.

Content change is change in the things we suffer from, pursue and grasp. In our youth we were just sure different content would make us happy and keep us happy. But it doesn't. It can't. Lasting happiness only comes from the shape of the bowl, the shape of the soul.

Which is why God answers just enough "me" prayers for us to learn how little lasting happiness a change in content brings.

But all along God is answering the "we" prayers by re-constructing and un-obstructing the structure of our souls.

Day 267

As God's workers, our job is to optimize the situations we find ourselves in. To optimize a situation means to increase as much as possible the stock of happiness in it that all can share.

It is not our place to complain and demand better situations. Why should we be exempt from bad situations? That would be coddling.

Instead, we pay close attention to the situation as it is, then pay close attention to God's ethical direction, then apply our guided attention and effort to the situation.

Things stop getting worse and start getting better. We bring justice with us. We act to make sure each creature gets what it needs to become what God intended it to become.

Day 268

We bring mercy with us. God was merciful to us and gave us a second chance. We know how many mistakes we made before we understood. We are patient with the mistakes others make when we see they are honestly trying to do better.

God gave us a margin for error while we were learning. We give others that same margin for error. We give them the benefit of the doubt.

Just as God gently came alongside us, we gently come alongside others.

We do not coddle, but we do not abandon others in their struggle either, just because it gets messy and discouraging.

Like God, we have high standards, but we are not cruel.

Day 269

There are situations with very little promise, but we optimize them anyway without complaining about the set up.

God never puts the cart before the horse.

God works first on our rate of optimization, then on how much or what we get to optimize.

If our rate of optimization remains the same and God places us in a content-rich situation, we will not see and optimize some of its possibilities. That would be wasteful. There is no waste in God's design.

We will optimize a content-rich situation at the same rate that we currently optimize a content- poor one.

Day 270

One tenant of God's happiness is optimizing any situation in which we find ourselves by multiplying its latent good possibilities.

What beavers and oak trees do for the place they inhabit we do for the lives we share a space with.

God didn't give us adaptable brains and opposable thumbs so we could enrich our lives at the expense of other lives from any species.

God gave us unique abilities to perform a unique function: to be the guardians of the current and future richness of life on earth.

Day 271

There are situations that cannot be optimized. These are organizations God will not renew or help optimize because humans intentionally built them to replace God, harm life and hoard resources.

These situations will change you before you change them.

God moves us out of those situations and on to more promising ones; even if we were born into them and know nothing else.

Guided by God, we learn when enough is enough. We are long-suffering but we are not fools.

Some of us must unlearn our tendency to leave too soon and some of us must unlearn our tendency to stay too long, but eventually we learn when to stay and when to leave, when to persist and when to quit.

Ironically, we become more influential after we are gone than we were when we were still around.

Those we have left come to realize things worked better when we were there.

They finally see the truth in what we were saying all along, even if it was not easy to understand at first, soothing or flattering.

Day 272

We are a migratory people. We function like the white blood cells in the body, ready to break camp and move to where God needs us next.

There are new situations that require our attention in another place.

God moves us there when it is time. It's ok. Our attachment to places and things is perforated, designed to break off with little effort when necessary.
We learn to let go graciously and travel light.

In contrast, our attachment to God and God's purposes is strong, designed to hold on tight through any circumstances we encounter. We carry light with us wherever we are sent.

Day 273

In our maturity we realize with awe and gratitude that God remembered our "we" prayers and promises.

God brought those deep aspirations into a daily, robust reality. That is how we know first-hand that God remembers.

Like the plant with its flower waiting for the bee, we can't know for sure, but it would be consistent with God's character to remember us after we are gone.

God has never abandoned us during our lives, nor did we abandon the thought of God through all those years, through all those struggles.

Why would God abandon the thought of us after we pass?

God is reciprocal.
God will not forget us.

It is another thing we have a deep learned confidence about that gives us contentment.

Staying close to God and fulfilling our calling, one life well lived is plenty.

We can face the final years of our lives in peace, then let go graciously.

We fear a life lived apart from God's direction, provision, and protection.

But we do not fear death because we know we will not be alone. God will meet us in our last moments just as God met us at every step along the way as we passed through every small death, every loss of what was never eternal to begin with.

Day 274

God designed the earth to provide well for all the life that exists and will exist in the future.

Plenty is God's plan. Hording disrupts God's plan and causes artificial scarcity. We fear diversity and try to drive out those who are different because we fear scarcity.

We fear there will not be enough for "us" if there is anything for "them." Or we fear "we" won't be able to fulfill our fantasies and get everything we want if "they" get everything they need.

Fear of scarcity and fear of diversity leads to the conclusion that uniformity in thought and behavior is the solution. The fear of difference fosters the paranoid idea that all our problems arose because we allowed that small group of different people to exist among us, even though they have done us no harm.

High organization with low diversity is a false complexity, and a fragile, false peace.

It is not God's peace. It is doomed.

Day 275

Monoculture is where only one type is allowed;
everything is the same. Monocultures collapse when a
pest or disease comes along that the uniform type can't
overcome.

In nature, life survives by producing an endless stream
of new options to manage situations that have not yet
developed but likely will. Diversity is how Life insures
itself.

We don't fear diversity of thought or lifestyle. We
protect it. It is from God. It is the glory of God and
reflects the divine genius embedded in Life.

Diversity helps fulfill the unique purpose earth serves in
the universe as one of the only places that can support
complex life. At least as far as we know.

At this writing we have found no other planet than can
support complex life.

How dare we suppress the very thing that sets our
planet apart? This party will not end well for humanity.

To enforce uniformity and unanimity is to mess with God's plans.

God will have the last word on that.

Day 276

So how do we respond to ideas and behaviors we don't agree with? We don't forbid bad ideas, we out-bid them. We point to a better alternative. But it must be proven to be better. That is only fair. We accept the challenge. It is the way of Life.

An idea is better if it can stand up to honest, logical scrutiny, if it lines up with what can be observed and measured over time. A better approach makes sense logically. The ideas in it fit together to form a whole.

An option is better when it works reliably. No matter who applies the new option or where they applied it, the results are better than with the old idea. In addition, those who apply the new, better approach find ways to make it work even better in even more situations.

When we rely upon a new idea to function better, and it does – we can have confidence we have found a new piece of structure, not just a new piece of content.

We can recommend the idea to others we care about knowing it will be helpful, not harmful.

Day 277

Just as it is thirst that makes cool, clean water so
refreshing, it is sustained experience with error that
makes truth so valuable once it is proven.
Error cannot stand up to scrutiny and will not function
as promised. Error will fail when it encounters
adversity. Truth grows clearer and stronger under the
pressure of adversity.

Our problem is not that we don't have truth available.
It is that we don't value it very much, so we let it go
without a struggle, allowing God's happiness to vanish
from the earth.

It is precisely the contrast with error and the results of
error that makes us finally see how uniquely valuable
God's happiness is.

Once we learn in our bones that God's happiness is far
more valuable than money and the things it can buy, no
longer can anyone buy or bribe us.

Day 278

There are those who say there is no truth, only points of view. The funny thing is they exempt that statement from their assertion that there is no truth. They demand that we accept as self-evident that there is no truth and start planning from there. It is a fraudulent scheme designed to entrap lazy, timid minds.

There is a truth about how trees grow and what they need to do so. That is not an opinion. There are no substitutes for what the tree needs. "Whatever" does not exist in nature. Take out phosphorus and plants can't grow. Trees grow straight up. There is one "up." It does not grow in "whatever" direction is popular this month.

God built the whole of creation on truths about what does and does not work. As part of creation, subject to all the forces and laws that govern everything else in creation, it is irrational to believe we can build our individual and collective happiness on "whatever" we find amusing or pleasurable at the moment, because it can't. Social structures built on popular fads collapse at the very moment they are most needed – in a crisis.

Day 279

Things fall apart. Everything goes from a higher to a lower state of order in a process called entropy. But in nature things also come together, moving from a lower to a higher state of order. This is a process called affinity.

In some unforeseen way, components somehow come together and somehow hold together. God's design harnesses the forces of entropy to create an order that keeps creating even higher order.

Only that which is participating in God's purposes demonstrates this amazing ability.

Only what God makes continually renews itself without just copying itself. Only what God makes keeps getting better. It is a process called virtue.

Virtue is what arrests and reverses entropy.

Things come together and hold together in ways we never could have planned. God's work is constantly new and surprising.

Day 280

Instead of coming together, godless endeavors come apart. Usually, things fall apart slowly in a way that is tedious and exhausting. There is nothing more discouraging than merely managing inevitable decline, fixing things that only break again.

Sometimes things fall apart in ways that are sudden and shocking.

When a civilization follows false signals it becomes like a speeding train, loaded with cargo. Each step leads naturally and logically to the next one, building up momentum. At some point it is almost impossible to slow down, re-direct, stop or get off. The passengers may not like what they must do next, but there is an internal logic in it all that requires the next move, even if it harms innocent lives that get in the way.
There comes a moment when the false signal demands a move over to a different, but parallel track, without slowing down.

In fact, everything speeds up using fancy new technology, following soothing new theories that promise a wonderful future.

All goes smoothly. The godless civilization seems to flourish once again.

Then something horrible happens.

Day 281

Just as God's happiness catches up to those who seek and follow God's ethical signal, God's misery catches up to those who refuse to do so.

Without realizing it they are now on the same track as an oncoming, fully loaded train.

There is room on the track for one train, but not two. The soothing theory did not account for two trains each pursuing the promised wonderful future at the same time.

When one godless endeavor collides head on with another godless endeavor or with unforeseen, natural events, everything that was built over decades or centuries vanishes in a fraction of the time it took to build.

A house that took the better part of a year to build, that was lived in, loved, and enhanced for 40 years can burn down in 4 hours, leaving nothing but ashes.

So it is with lives, careers, endeavors, empires. and entire civilizations.

Day 282

God's justice catches up to those who violate the laws of life. It happens when the natural built-in consequences of one's choices collide with a rare, unforeseen development in the larger situation.

When epochal changes occur the only safe place to be is on God's side of the contest. But it takes decades to learn how to stay on God's side no matter what happens, no matter what the cost. We can't just switch trains once we realize we made a huge mistake. Humans can mislead each other, but not God.

We can't just switch to "whatever" we like, "whenever" we feel like it, at a time and place that is convenient for us. Even though religious merchants promise otherwise, we can't just go shopping for a novel approach to God, certain some merchant has already provided an easy, quick, pleasant fix.

It doesn't work that way. It is too late.

There was always in fact only one right track to be on: on God's side in every ethical debate, and by God's side to receive constant corrective guidance.

Day 283

Everything the godless gained by ignoring God they lose in the collision and the firestorm it causes.

The godly are also impacted by the effects of what the godless put in play. Somehow enough of the godly escape with their lives, their mutual aid relationships, and their wisdom, but little else.

That is why the godly learn not to hoard and cling to possessions, positions, or institutions.

They always knew someday it would all burn. They placed their trust elsewhere.

As always, the godly find they have enough in hand to begin again, but this time to build something new and totally different.

Day 284

Who waits on whom? The one with less knowledge waits to see the one with more knowledge. The one with less power waits to see the one with more power. I don't set the conditions for seeing my doctor. The doctor does.

God does not wait on us. We wait on God. Just because we come to appreciate the vast difference between ourselves and God does not mean we need someone to talk to God for us, it just means we must learn how to behave ourselves before the Highest Authority.

We seek God when and where God may be found. That time and place is up to God. We pay whatever price we must pay. There may well be only one chance to get on the right track. If we miss it the moment passes and could never come again.

It has happened to others in history. There are no deathbed conversions. What good would that do?

Conversions happen while we still have time to live different lives, or not at all. The moment of meeting God will never be convenient, chosen by us, easy, cheap, or managed by another human.

True conversions only happen in dumbstruck solitude between us and our Creator, most often inspired by and enveloped in the majesty of nature.

True conversion leads us to devote our entire lives to God's purposes on earth. Last minute conversions are not a gimmick to hedge our bets just in case there is a God who is just. We don't expect God to reward those who bring their burnt-out leftovers the same as those who bring the best they have for as long as they've got. To do so would be unjust. To teach that God would do so and call it "forgiveness" is to slander God's character.

In nature a creature that never learns how to survive as a constructive member of a social species forfeits the protection and support of its group – and dies earlier and uglier than it would have otherwise.

True conversions happen early enough in our lives to make a pivotal difference in how we invest the best and bulk of our time, attention and talents.

Day 285

To follow God's ethical signal, we will have to leave behind other things, big things.

Why?

We determine the value of something by what we are willing to give up to obtain or experience it.

If we are unwilling to give up anything to establish a stable directing signal with God, we are saying very clearly that there are things more valuable than a stable connection to God.

That is a lie. That lie will put us on the wrong track.

Day 286

Stable, daily contact with God will be the solution to all your problems. But staying in contact with God will become the problem to all your solutions, and the solutions of your social group.

Just as before all the noise of the culture drowned out the quiet ethical signal from God, God's signal will disrupt and displace the signals of the culture. We start to see how false and dangerous it was all along.

The structural rebuilding has begun. Your soul comes alive. Your eyes and ears are opened. Your words and actions, your thoughtless neglect all start to matter. You take care in ways you never had time for before.
You take care of things you never thought mattered before. You notice people you ignored before.

Day 287

Earth is the name of our home. "World" is the name of the contrived reality humans have built on lies about God, lies about famous people and lies about nature.

As God rebuilds us we become less worldly and more earthly. We become what God designed us to be – godly earthlings at home on earth, not at war with it.

The lives around us start to feel at home with us. When any creature feels safe and provided for, its natural strengths emerge. It will start to do what comes naturally, what it was made to do. Our consistent kindness, attention, and carefulness create a safe, nutrient-rich habitat for other lives.

Habitat is the place where a creature can express instinctive behaviors safely, sensing that when it does it will benefit. Even without intending to, its behaviors benefit the lives around it.

We thrive together or we die together. It is natural.

Day 288

Humans are the only species that can use tools to measure whether Earth is thriving or dying and use language to work together to do something about it. Humans who are connected to God, that is – godly earthlings.

Disconnected from God, we are no longer fully human, so we can't and won't perform the vital monitoring and cultivating function God intended.

Disconnected from God's ethical signal we cease to be earthlings, becoming proud and worldly. We think we are better and smarter than trees or beavers. We trust dead machines more than life. We value money over love.

In time worldlings come to value most precisely the things life abhors. Then they succumb to delusions and throw themselves into frantic efforts to turn their fantasies into reality.

The worldly path always ends in some form of madness.

Day 289

Proud worldlings can see that the earth is dying but can't do anything about it. Worldlings can't close ranks to solve common problems because each individual and each group is chasing a private fantasy, using private magic to build a private surplus at the expense of everyone else.

Each group thinks if *they* are OK *everything* is OK.

But everything is clearly not OK. And everything depends upon – everything.

Proud worldlings are today's "winners" – but will be the ultimate losers.

Humble earthlings are today's "losers" – but will be the ultimate winners.

Day 290

Our brains sit enclosed inside our skulls. To function, the brain must take in environmental information from the senses, then create a rough model of what is going on outside the skull.

Then the brain figures out what to do next, working within this constructed model.

It is in modelling reality that things break down, where we can lose contact with God and become doomed worldlings.

If we construct the model out of wishes and fantasies we start sleepwalking through our habitat, harming lives, including our own.

The marks of sleepwalking are certainty, superiority, rigidity, and aggression.

Day 291

When our mental model of reality is informed by history and constructed from careful and patient observation, measurement, and testing, we lose the delusion of certainty and superiority. We realize there is far more we don't know than we do know.

The best way to make sure our mental models are the closest possible approximation to reality is to seek and use feedback from reality.

Feedback will expose magical thinking and remove delusions.

We use our own personal history, the one we know best. In God's natural way of acquiring reliable knowledge, we put words and deeds into the world and see what happens in response.

We take in the information that comes out of our experiments and ask God for guidance. Then we use God's guidance to adjust our next set of words and deeds. Then we see if the outcome is better and are honest with ourselves about what we see.

With each round we become more precise and more ethical. Those who learn nothing from their own history, or from the history of their group, are sleepwalking down the wrong track.

Day 292

Once we appreciate how complex and fluid reality is, we realize we need a greater Mind than our own to responsibly map and engage reality.

God does not call us to be optimistic, but to be realistic and ethical. We are realistic if we know our limits and stay within them. That is all humility is. It is not self-deprecation.

We are not omniscient. We need information from The One who is.

Day 293

We are not God. We can't know future unforeseen events. We can't predict unintended consequences. We can't read the thoughts and intentions of others. We can't even know for sure why things happened in the past if enough time has elapsed. Records get lost and memories dim.

God's ethical guiding signal enters our honest but incomplete internal model and informs our deliberations using experiments and feedback.

In the face of uncertainty, doing nothing is not always the best strategy. "Do nothing" is the motto of the lazy coward.

No creature in nature seeks to do nothing, or else its kind would have already gone extinct.

Rather, in nature, when creatures face unfamiliar situations they immediately begin the work of finding out what is the best thing to do, ready to do it when the time is right,.

We often can't know for sure what choice is best, but we can always seek guidance from the One who does.

We cry out for help. We fall silent. We watch. We listen. God guides by gentle touch and a kind whisper.

Peace displaces anxiety.

Sometimes we break into spontaneous laughter. Sometimes we are moved to tears of grateful joy. Sometimes we fall silent in complete awe of God's genius.

Day 294

We can't make God into anything we want. God is what God is. We can't relate to God any way we want, but that does not mean we can't directly relate to God. We can and we must.

We must relate to God as God and nothing else, and nothing less. But there is nothing better on earth than relating to God the way God requires.

No one can do this for you. Don't let them try. Just because God is vast and mysterious does not mean you need a go-between. It just means you must approach in profound respect.

The only way to relate to God is directly, personally, in solitude, intending to hear and promptly obey ethical guidance.

Once we have clear ethical guidance we don't put off acting on it. Delayed obedience is disobedience.

God does not help the disobedient. There is no lasting happiness or effectiveness without God's help.

Day 295

Receiving God's guiding signal will require logic. Logic drives out magic as light drives out darkness. We don't ignore verifiable facts. We think through the likely consequences of our actions or inaction. Regardless of how strongly we feel about a contested value, we are responsible for the consequences of our actions. We can't ignore that.

We become careful and helpful. We lose our rigidity. Our plans become limited and fluid, open to current information and a better approach. Rivals become partners. Resisters become assisters.

We do things that have no precedent, but fit the situation, while embodying a strong goodness. God's presence and wisdom enters the situation and changes everything.

Day 296

Separate from God our models of reality are fantasies; our behaviors are rigid or random. Our attitudes are callous or frivolous. Our faces grow tight and lifeless. Our words are cutting.

Connected to God our models of reality become accurate enough to inform ethical decisions. Our behaviors are original and adaptive. Our attitudes are gentle. Our faces are soft and carry a warm glow, reflecting the One we spend time with. Our words are gracious.

Like a wonderful piece of music our decisions and solutions have components that are new, surprising, and necessary to make it all work. Maturity can be more fun than adolescence.
With God as our trainer, adulthood recaptures the wonder of childhood.

Day 297

Our inspired lives become a note in the vast symphony of creation. We do what God created us to do in the time and place God assigns to us.

We take our place alongside God's other masterpieces. There is no greater honor.

It makes no difference how many people notice. It is not about fame; it is about fit.

As a pollinator, there is no question that a hummingbird fits into life on earth. Although it is small, in its beauty and function it still rivals all the productions humans have ever created combined.

Even if no one ever sees the butterfly, it is no less wonderful and essential.

Day 298

Following God's ethical guidance we relearn...

When we are dependent and how to behave in those situations.

When we are independent and how to behave in those situations.

When we are interdependent and how to behave in those situations.

Clarity about these three states leads to God's happiness.

Confusion about these three states leads to needless suffering. That suffering is what prompts us to start the relearning process.

Day 299

Factually and logically, if I owe my original existence to another's actions, I am dependent on that other one. If I did nothing to earn it, I am the recipient of grace – undeserved favor.

If I owe my continued existence to what another provides, I am dependent on that other one.

If I cannot do what I need to do without information, resources, or power held by another, I am dependent on that other one.

If there is no way I can provide the information, resources, or power I need for myself, no matter how hard I work or what technique I use – I am in a dependent state.

Any notion that tells me otherwise is a dangerous fantasy.

It is best to get on with learning how to behave any time I am legitimately and inescapably dependent rather than waste time and energy pretending otherwise.

If the dependency I am experiencing comes from force or fraud it is neither necessary nor legitimate. Yet I remain enslaved.

I need to learn what to do to restore my God given independence.

Day 300

I am dependent upon God for my existence. I did not create myself or the planet I live on.

I am dependent upon nature for my existence. I cannot produce my own air, water, or gravity.

I am dependent upon God's unlimited knowledge when facing any unknown, fluid, ambiguous situation.

When there is no way I can know for sure know how things will turn out, I am dependent on the One who does know.

Day 301

I am dependent upon others for my care and protection when I am an infant, a child, sick, injured or very old. Others around me will be dependent on me when they are in one of those states. Those are temporary states. If I have a disability I may be partially or completely dependent on others my entire life.

In managing the life cycle, we learn to be interdependent. In taking care of those who cannot take care of themselves we learn to pay attention, to be patient and compassionate, to take turns, to share, to cooperate and collaborate.

When we are interdependent we learn to create arrangements of mutual aid that are easy and natural to maintain.

We never ask for aid without looking for a way to give aid in return, even if it takes years to do so.

We can fix our mutual aid arrangements when they break down because we built them ourselves.

Day 302

I am in an interdependent relationship when I take care of a living ecosystem that provides for my physical needs. In doing so I learn the art of husbandry.

I come to understand the nature of a living thing before attempting to care for it. I don't impose my wishes on it. I learn to see as many of the interdependencies as I can in the habitat to make sure I don't disrupt them. Everything depends upon everything around it.

I am learning carefulness. I learn sequences, amounts and intricate timing. I learn the moods and seasons of those I care for, who also take care of me.

I learn all of this by direct observation and practice.

As a restored earthling, I behave like a skilled musician in a great orchestra.

I find awe, meaning and joy in being part of it all rather than having control over it all.

Day 303

Only when I have learned legitimate dependence and interdependence have I earned the legitimate right to some independence, because I won't abuse it.

I now know experientially that God is God, nature provides, and I need the support of others to survive, or I will someday soon.
Without needing permission or intervention from any other human, I make daily, direct contact with God. No one can control or forbid that. No one has the right to do so. If anyone tries, I assert my God-given independence.

Day 304

I work to support myself and those I love, by bringing in income and/or by doing chores. If I am not in one of the legitimately dependent states mentioned earlier, I am not entitled to the support of others. I don't expect others to breathe for me or walk for me, why would I expect others to pay my bills or do my chores?

God has given me the local, immediate resources I need. I can access them in exchange for labor. The more useful my labor is, the more resources I can access. If I pay attention I will see God-given opportunities to make my labor more useful to others.

It is my duty to make the most of the opportunities around me, to cultivate my abilities, and to access the resources God placed in my situation. No mature creature in nature is hand-fed.

I don't ask God to give me money without effort, and I don't seek or accept money from others without providing real service in return. I don't gain resources by taking away what God provided for other creatures.

I do not practice magic or fraud. I do not hoard.

Day 305

To solve a problem no one can solve alone, we form mutual support arrangements. We know we need each other. We interact with each other to make our own decisions. We sometimes seek or accept solutions from others far away who do not know our situation firsthand, but only after we have made full use of the information we already have, waiting to be discovered.

We have no need for a historic link to somebody thousands of years ago that gives our group legitimacy. There is a simple rule of thumb: any person who will not show up to help when we need to move from one dwelling to another cannot tell us how to solve real problems in our situation.

Mindlessly deferring to a faraway authority or celebrity is a false dependency that exists nowhere in nature. My immune system does not wait until my doctor tells it what to do. It responds immediately to a pathogen with what it has in hand. In a similar way, a direct two-way link to God and nature is in our DNA and older than any human institution, and it is more than sufficient to guide our decision-making process today, right where we are.

Day 306

We assert our independence when our ability to respond to the situations we face is obstructed. We cry out to God for guidance and help.

God meets, teaches us, and aids us in this struggle. It is this very struggle for natural, local independence that restores God's design for earth.

Groups solve bigger problems than individuals can.
God made us to cooperate with each other.
Cooperation is our greatest power. No one has the right to get in the way.

We accept the awesome responsibility of freedom; we don't flee it.
We don't give our responsibility away to others because we are not children.

Day 307

Those who forfeit or substitute their legitimate dependency on God lose it, and with it, God's direction, provision, and protection. Like everything truly priceless, once God's direction is lost it is so difficult to regain - few if any ever do.

Those who neglect or disrupt the legitimate interdependency God designed to exist between creatures lose all the benefits and joys of interdependence. Those trying to create alone, what can only be created in cooperation with others, fall into the lethal quicksand of loneliness. Few if any ever escape.

Those who don't fight to keep their God given independence lose it. They become enslaved, and their lives will be used to further other people's goals, not God's goals. Few if any will ever breathe the fresh air of freedom again.

God's happiness catches up with and envelops the lives of those who learn to be willingly dependent on God's guidance,

God's happiness catches up with and thrills the soul of those who learn to be helpfully interdependent with others whom God placed in their lives,

God's happiness catches up with and strengthens those who learn to be fiercely independent both morally, materially and intellectually in order to remain free and available for God's purposes.

Day 308

The vast majority of humans have chosen the path to extinction by choosing not to participate in life on life's terms. We have not. We have chosen the path of protection, renewal, and restoration.

It is a path we discover on our own, then group up and build out together. Each of us, and each of our groups, starts out from a different place, but we are all headed in the same direction.

The diversity of initial conditions requires a diversity of different paths forward.

Our work makes it possible and more likely for others to follow later, no matter where they start from. We accelerate their journey by laying the groundwork and leaving behind reliable road signs.

Those who come after us find our observations were accurate, and our reasoning was sound.
They will reciprocate by picking up where we leave off.

They will correct our errors and surpass us.

Day 309

It is very fulfilling to see those we helped go farther and do better work than we ever could have done.

We don't want those who come after us to worship us and live for our purposes. We are mere creatures. We want them to know and worship God and live for their Creator's purposes, which are still unfolding.

Yet they will feel their sense of indebtedness to us and repay us by doing the same for those who come after them. There is no higher honor.

We cooperate across generations in a constant unfolding of unforeseen wonders, not a constant repeating of dead traditions.
It is the way of Life and the glory of God.

Day 310

When it is time to organize, we take time to study how nature organizes. Why replicate human forms of organization that have caused more problems than they solved? Nature's solutions dwarf ours in scale, effectiveness, and longevity. Nature's solutions are both beautiful and functional.

In nature we see open structures. Open structures are marvels of interdependence; they cannot exist without effectively interacting with their environments.

An open structure is a kind of enriching pass-through. It takes in energy, materials, and information, then combines them to put something back into the environment.

Other living things either find useful what the open structure produced, or they don't.

If the environment finds its output useful, the open structure draws in more energy, materials, and information.

Both the open structure and its environment benefit and thrive.

Day 311

In nature we see open structures emerge locally and spontaneously over a wide expanse of territory. Forests are a good example. Each one is autonomous and self-sustaining, adjusting to what happens around it. It does not wait for direction or permission from some other creature.

Small units, widely distributed, that link up into a larger network is the norm in long-lived ecosystems.

In our bodies the digestive, respiratory, and excretory systems facilitate the intake and output of substances from outside themselves and each system helps keep the others functioning.

The combination of open structures and wide distribution optimizes both local innovation and collective effort. The larger collective does not stifle individual initiative or differences in opinion and form. The individual does not harm the local open structure or the larger network, taking more than it gives.

Individuals do not grow at the expense of the group and groups do not sustain themselves at the expense of the individual's unique development.

In nature we see both high differentiation of parts and high integration of all the parts into a complex and dynamic whole.

There is constant, necessary, creative tension between individual and group needs, but eventually the needs of both individuals and the group as whole are met. If they were not, the system would collapse.

Day 312

A clock is an enclosed system. It receives energy from outside to run, but then nothing outside itself influences what it does or how it does it. This might work for a lifeless machine, but it does not work for a living society. Every attempt to turn people into parts of a lifeless machine has ended tragically.

We don't create enclosed social structures because we must keep pace with God to be useful to God. What we might gain in permanence we lose in relevance.

For the soul, any enclosed structure starts to feel like an elegant museum at best, a prison at worst. We are not dead artifacts, so we don't need to live our lives in a museum. We have been liberated by God, so we don't need to live our lives in a prison.

Enclosed structures form blockages that prevent us from moving on and changing. When we stop moving into new situations our brains wither away.

At best, books, buildings, and rituals may point toward God, but are too static to guide us through the current situation, which is always unique in some way.

We must love God more than even the most cherished human tradition. Divided loyalty is disloyalty. To be ethical and intellectually honest, there comes a time when we must grow beyond any tradition and learn to follow God directly.

God's unfolding design is too big, too fluid, to be bottled for convenience. We look for things that function more like a windsock than a clock because it never loses contact with its surrounding situations. And windsocks never lie.

Day 313

God uses nature, history, and our conscience to teach us how to behave as part of earth.

Why nature? Because we need models to inform our mental models. Nature is full of working models of diversity and cooperation, adaptation, and replacement.

Why history? Because God have humans the freedom to choose. History is the record of how choices turn out over time. History is the story of freedom used well and used badly. Everything you see has a history.

Why conscience? To have a soul is to feel empathy. We sense that if someone did to us what we are contemplating, it would feel hateful. It could be harmful, so we don't do it.

The pain of empathy stops us in our tracks. We cry out to God and seek another way to solve our problem. We stay open.

We avoid those who demonstrate rigidity and a lack of conscience because connection is contagion.

We don't want their values to become ours.

Day 314

We build open structures. We take in information, energy and resources and then combine them into actions that meet our needs while enriching the habitat we share with other creatures. Open structures require feedback loops to function.

The most accurate measure of a group's health is how long it takes to stop doing something hurtful or useless.

We are honest about how our decisions work out, so we stop doing things that don't work or harms others. We quickly acknowledge there is something wrong, this isn't working, this does not honor God. As a group, we stop, regroup, and aim higher.

We propose a better way to understand our situation based on observation and reason.

We propose an experiment to see if we are getting closer to the truth.
We live experimentally.

As our own lives become an adventure of discovery, we have less need for entertainment.

Day 315

When there are more and different lives, all thriving together, benefiting each other precisely because they are different from each other, we know we are getting closer to the truth about God's design. The closer we get to God's design for earth, the closer God's happiness gets to us.

On the other hand, when we see there are fewer and more similar lives, having the same conversation about the same topics, we know have gotten on the wrong track. Like a stagnant and polluted pond, enclosed structures give off the stench of predictability, certainty, and tedium.

Rather than copying the past, we wipe the slate clean and begin again. We invite new minds to the table.

They were there all along, but because they are different and have different ideas we left them out and never considered their needs.

Day 316

False superiority is thinking every possible combination has been tried when it hasn't. There is an unforeseen component the newcomer or outsider brings to the table.

Like a steady stream of clean water hitting a stagnant pond, this open, welcoming, constant flow of better ways flushes out older ones. This allows us to correct and surpass what we did before.

We appreciate those who went before, but we do not worship them or their work. They are not God.

Yesterday's solutions cannot solve today's problems. In fact, yesterday's solutions are the most frequent root cause of today's problems.

Our connection to the Creator allows us to do more than maintain what others made. We can participate in creating things that have never existed before to fit situations that have never existed before.

Day 317

We don't gather in large groups in one place. We do not form huge crowds listening to one person. God does not distribute guidance and skills for living that way.

We do not create centralized organizations where decisions are made at the center and resources are distributed from the center.

Centralized systems do not exist in nature for a reason. They don't survive. Once an anti-social sickness enters a centralized system, which will always happen, it spreads to the entire organization.

Units far from the center are sickened and paralyzed but can do nothing to cure the disease flowing from the center.

In our distributed system we can nip in the bud an anti-social sickness as soon as it appears in our local group. God expects us to do just that. If we don't, other distributed units can quickly sever ties with us to prevent infection. The sickness is quarantined and dies out.

Stages attract actors. Large audiences attract narcissists who just want to be the center of attention, in place of God. We don't let that sickness get started. With no stages, no audiences and no actors, there will be fewer if any actions done just for show.

Day 318

If the center distributes resources, it can control what goes on by threatening to withhold resources. A centralized system always creates unnatural dependence, fawning, and palace politics.

Our distributed units remain independent, providing for itself making the most of the local resources God entrusted to us. Our groups may be small, and they may not have fancy things, but they are nimble and fast. We set our own standards and then enforce them. We make our own plans and then implement them. We run our own experiments and then evaluate them. That is nature's freedom, the freedom to thrive.

Being told what we can and can't do by those who don't share our situation is forced stupidity. Forced stupidity is a form of slavery.

No slave can be very happy for long.
We are not slaves and will not be enslaved.

Day 319

In natural networks, God's intelligence is added all along every pathway of life. In unnatural networks, intelligence is concentrated at the center, at the top.

Unnatural networks punish and remove intelligence that shows up farther down the line. Unnatural, centralized systems say to everyone below the top "we think – you do. Stop it! You're thinking! That's our job. Do what we tell you."

Groups honoring God's design ask those who have proven themselves to be helpful, "what do you think? How can we best cultivate rich diversity and high cooperation right here, right now?"

In natural organizations each local unit seeks God's direction to find new and better ways to be more productive, using fewer resources, to solve more problems in their own particular situation.

Day 320

False religions say the proof of divine presence is miracles and that a miracle is when something that does not happen in nature happens, as if God got it wrong when setting up nature.

The idea behind chasing this kind of "miracle" is magic. When what normally takes time, attention and effort happens instantly, easily, without paying close attention for a long time – God must be involved. Apparently, since normally making wine takes time, when someone turns into wine quickly, God must be present.

It takes years of training, discipline, and patience to make wine. God encourages those virtues; God does not upstage them.

A true miracle is when something that has happened on rare occasions in nature or history happens again at a crucial moment in the struggle between honoring and ignoring God's design for our lives on Earth.

A miracle has occurred when completely unforeseen and unplanned, a power greater than the combatants enters the fray on the side of the just.

A miracle can happen in the intimacy of single life or in the drama of a world war, but in either case what was impossible before suddenly becomes possible.

A miracle is a natural event that creates an opening in the situation that was not there before, at exactly the place and time in which such an opening was most needed.

Day 321

God's involvement is not marked by that fact that things suddenly become fast, easy, and pleasurable.

God's involvement is marked by the fact that injustice is being replaced by justice. Justice is never fast or easy. God is present in the struggle to create and protect justice.

Justice is a way of relating to life that makes sure every creature has what it needs to fulfill God's purpose for its existence. Justice alone produces high diversity and high cooperation.

The experience of justice after a long period of injustice fills us with relief, gratitude, happiness, pleasure and delight just as getting water to a drought-ravaged wasteland can trigger a cascade of new unfolding life.

There is nothing more miraculous than a thriving, natural ecosystem. Learning about true complexity sets a new, high standard that must be met before we call something miraculous.

Day 322

God's happiness is all about relearning how to use our two most precious gifts: our time and attention. Time and attention are precious because they are powerful, and we only have so much of each.

Convenience is the idea that the world should be arranged so that we get what we want using as little time and attention as possible, because we have more important things to do with the rest of our time and attention.

A zoo is an artificial world arranged so that people can see bored but healthy animals - conveniently. Seeing the same animals thriving in their natural habitat, by struggling with all the things that threaten their survival, would require an extravagant expenditure of time, money, and attention. It is inconvenient to observe and absorb the truth.

Day 323

God will not be put on display in a zoo. God will not show up and perform in a specific building on a pre-scheduled day at a pre-scheduled time so humans can conveniently get a non-disruptive, soothing, mood elevating dose of God, then go back to behaving the way they were, hoping to do better but knowing it's not a problem if they don't.

God is not a zoo animal or circus act. We do not attempt to enclose and schedule God for convenient consumption like any other product. We adjust to God's requirements; we do not even suggest that God should adjust to ours.

A naturalist pays the price in decades of study and careful observation then gets to see a creature do what comes naturally and learn its patterns of relating productively to the lives around it.

We too get to witness God's wisdom in action because we paid attention in the real world for as long as it took no matter how inconvenient it was to do so. It is only fair. It is a natural consequence of investing our time and attention in ways few others have.

We are no longer speculating or repeating ancient speculations about God. We are eyewitnesses to God's majestic genius in action.

When asked, the word of an eyewitness carries weight in a way that hearsay does not.

Day 324

We can't cooperate with God's wisdom until we have seen it in action.

Once we have seen God's wisdom in action in nature, in history, and in our own souls we are more likely to see opportunities to extend God's ruling wisdom to our relationships, right where we are.

The inconvenience of the work verifies that it is real. We don't mind because this is the way God's vast intelligence is distributed all along the network of living relationships.

God brings justice back to earth one unnoticed, inconvenient interaction at a time.

Day 325

Most of a river's water is subterranean, flowing below the surface parallel to the flow above. When rivers dry out on the surface, there is still water underneath, which can gurgle up again farther down the parched riverbed. Once water is flowing again on the surface, systems of life naturally emerge again.

In the same way, humanity will not be redeemed from the top down, from the many, the powerful, and the famous. Humanity will be redeemed from the bottom up, from the few, the simple, the invisible and ignored.

God's rule will return from deep inside individuals and from within the practical, problem-solving fellowship of small local groups governed by God, not by huge organizations with grand plans.

It will be clear whose genius was at work: God's. No other explanation will make sense.

We won't feel great happiness because we have a great leader.

We will feel great happiness because we will know God is in charge.

Day 326

When we transfer our responsibility for contact with
God to an institution we leave a vast and growing
vacuum in our souls.

When we transfer our responsibility to create justice to
impersonal bureaucracies we leave a vast and growing
vacuum in our communities.
Nature abhors a vacuum; it will be filled with
something. The same thing happens with the soul and
with communities. What can fill a vast and growing
vacuum, but a vast and growing madness?

Fantasy, magic, self-absorption, games, rivalries, and
resentments rush in to take the place of our
responsibilities to God, to earth and to each other,
pushing out God's happiness.
When we hold on to our responsibilities, it leaves no
place for evil to take root and God's happiness stays
with us.

Day 327

We retain personal responsibility for the quality of our relationship with God and the experience we create for the other lives that share our space.
Personal responsibility is the name we use for the space we hold in our hearts and lives for God. God fills the space with a different personal happiness made up of...

Contentment,
triumph, joy, meaning,
freedom, effectiveness, togetherness, gratitude,
sound sleep, variety, play, wonder, spontaneity,
excitement...

and the list keeps getting longer and longer...

God is so good.

So very, truly good.

Day 328

We retain a sense of shared responsibility for how our group treats others and uses its resources. Shared responsibility is the name we use for the space we hold in common for God's presence among us.

God fills the space with a different happiness made up of...

Mutual support,
cooperation, reciprocity,
resourcefulness, efficiency, inventiveness
belonging, safety, goodwill, loyalty, elegance,
relevance..... and the list just keeps getting longer.

There is so much goodness under God's rule. There is no scarcity. Goodness overflows. When we share our joy it only grows, there is no less for others and other groups.

Our corner of earth rebounds and rejoices, under our care.

God welcomes us home.

Day 329

God's happiness is a different happiness, and it comes into our lives differently.

God's happiness enters, rules, and makes us into a different kind of person.

We pair up differently with others of our kind.
We put together working groups of our kind in a different way.

Our collective happiness is so different we preserve it differently.

We pass on our different happiness in a different way.

Why is there so much difference? Because we are called to be a break in the patterns of human civilization, not an extension of those patterns.

Day 330

Where God rules directly in individual souls, a new society can begin.

In history, we find colonies established by empires. In nature we find colonies established by life.

Imperial colonies are small copies of the imperial capital. Natural colonies are typically a species that came from another place, repeating in a new place what it did in its previous place.

In both cases the colony is an extension, a continuation of what already exists.

But there are rare original colonies in both human and natural history. Original colonies make a clean break from what went before.

Original colonies are working experiments where something new, different, and better is taking form.

We are working models. Working is the key word. Why so much work? Because before a better way of living on earth can take hold, it must first show that it works by surviving through times of real, not imagined adversity.

Once proven better, the better way never stops improving itself.

The carriers of God's happiness are a new original human colony.

We don't follow the old rules that don't work.

We write new ones that do work.

Day 331

In the world's happiness, words get far ahead of deeds.
Deeds never quite catch up. Religions, philosophies,
and forms of government make big promises but never
actually deliver on their promises even after thousands
of years and millions of attempts. It was a mirage all
along.

We use the opposite approach.
In our happiness, since it is about continuous work,
deeds get way ahead of words. Go study the ocean.
There is SO much going on all at once. Some of it has
been observed and described, but most of it hasn't.
Even what has been put down in words is quickly out of
date because the ocean has changed and has produced
something new.

So it is with us. We are a mystery to others. They can
tell something qualitatively different is happening.

But they can't explain it, and we aren't talking. We are
too busy doing.

Often what we are experiencing is so amazing it lies
beyond the holding capacity of language. We struggle
for adequate words, leaving us stammering.

Even if we could talk about it happening in and around us we would be met with incredulous disbelief. But were words fail us, deeds do not.

Day 332

Few things are as attractive as a genuine mystery. Our lives contain the answers to questions others have not yet learned to ask. They have been working on the wrong questions.

Our work does more than achieve an outcome others can't achieve. Our work achieves an outcome others can't imagine. They have long since settled for far too little.

We are a mysterious, hidden people. We don't put ourselves or our ways on display. We don't run a zoo. We put ourselves and our ways into projects that produce better results.

Like any other work of nature, we cause the WHY question to arise in the honest mind with a sensitive conscience.

Day 333

The most reliable guide to action is experience. In unprecedented situations the very thing we lack is experience. Speculation, hearsay, and theory are not substitutes for experience; in fact, it is dangerous to act on those things.

The way we give ourselves experience is to organize small, local, risk-managed experiments. We are in uncharted territory and have no instruction manual. The situation is not static but changing as we speak. There is little we can know for sure. The situation is indefinite and emerging.

It is precisely on the frontier, in situations that have not yet been defined, where the rules have not yet been worked out, that we find the greatest range of creative possibilities.

The indefinite, the zone beyond the known, is the natural habitat for any creative mind.

God is the greatest creative mind.
When we become comfortable around the indefinite we have entered God's inner chamber, the room where what really matters unfolds.

Day 334

We are an experimental human colony. We hold a divine charter. We work under God's direction.

We can't know for sure ahead of time what we will become or what we will create, nor do we need to. We don't control the agenda.

We stand ready for whatever needs to be done. Our job is to stay fit to function well as an experimental colony. That is no easy task.
Unusual work requires an unusual code of conduct.

We have a few functional values that make sure we remain an open and distributed unit. We don't commit these values to books, we commit them to memory because they must become reflexive behaviors for us.

Writing down rules of conduct only makes us think we have arrived and invites selfish minds to find the loopholes.

Day 335

We don't trust lectures or sermons to embed our values in our hearts. The way we embed values proves their value. It is the way life lessons are passed on in nature from parent to offspring - by modeling, observation, and mimicking.

We embed the sustaining values of our colony in real lives. We have living examples among us who consistently do well things that matter. If we imitate them we won't be too far off course.

There is a short list of things our role models never do, always do, and do differently. These reflexive behaviors set us apart and keep us useful to God.
Within these behavioral limits there is freedom to try anything that might increase the stock of happiness on earth for all life.

Day 336

We are gracious. Courtesy is natural to us because we are agents of the Highest Court. We are not rude to each other. We don't interrupt, we listen.

We don't tear each other down; we build each other up. We love to see every member of the colony growing in uniqueness, confidence and competence, willing to take on new and harder tasks.

We are polite. We say "please" when we request help, "thank you" when we receive help, and "sorry" when we have been unhelpful for any reason.

Politeness is a social lubricant. It keeps things from getting too hot in the friction that comes with working hard together.

We are truthful. We don't reveal everything we know, but we don't knowingly mislead each other.

Day 337

We are conscientious. We take our responsibilities seriously, managing our time and attention to get done what we have promised to do. We follow up on conversations and follow through on promises.

We are very hospitable. We are never hostile to strangers just for being different or having different ideas.

We never know what God may have sent our way through a stranger. We delight in the richness of God's variety.

Day 338

We are curious. The universe is a vast mystery. We don't pretend we are perfect and know everything. We are humbled by all we don't know, and even more by what we don't know we don't know.

We remain open to correction and improvement from any source that is true to life. Trusting curiosity is the natural response of an intelligent creature when touching the genius of creation.

We communicate more through deeds than words. Observing God's wordless works is what won our trusting admiration to begin with. In turn we don't ask others to trust our words in lieu of results.

We focus on results because they speak eloquently for themselves.

We also will not allow anyone to deny our results and ignore our words, when we have more experience with a problem than they do.

We seek God's guidance, then apply an appropriate consequence when others deny what is true about us and our work.

Applying consequences is not being selfish or petty. It would be unethical to not warn others when our deep experience tells us they are in danger if they do not change course.

We are quiet much of the time. Creativity requires slow thinking and slow thinking takes time, quiet time. We protect the solitude and quiet time of others so they can seek God. We don't fill the air with noise or chatter just to pass the time.

Long pauses are normal in nature.

Day 339

We are collaborative. We work hard together to arrive at new and better solutions. We are hard on the problem but soft on each other.

We work hard to keep our relationships happy because we will work soon together on something else.

We are disciplined in our assertiveness, placing assertiveness within healthy boundaries.

Each of us thinks, "my needs are just as important as yours, but no more, and no less. I am not passive; I do not believe your needs matter and mine don't. I am not aggressive; I do not believe my needs matter and yours don't." Both aggression and passivity destroy any enjoyment of "we." Healthy, gracious assertiveness enriches the experience of "we."

Working collaboratively, we take care of what takes care of us. We never exploit, ruin, and then abandon a natural space. We make sure it is even healthier for all lives that will live there in the future.

Day 340

The most precious resource our colony has is its attention. We gather and focus our collective attention on the challenges facing us in our situation. Our values optimize our individual and collective attention by guiding us to the most reliable sources of direction.

We direct attention up to God, out to nature, back to history and within to our individual consciences. From these sources we find clues. We find keys that open boxes of keys.

Over time, through conversations that last years, we piece together the clues and find new paths to new solutions.

Day 341

Because God is present with us here, now, in our current situation, we don't need to direct undue attention to any person alive today or who lived in the past.

We don't allow a cult of personality to grow around anyone among us. No one who loves God hordes attention or leadership. Rather, one who loves God directs attention to God and shares leadership.

We function like migrating geese. One takes the lead for a set amount of time to break the wind resistance and make it easier for those farther back in the formation. Then that leader falls back to the rear and another, more rested one takes the lead.

We regularly pass the baton of leadership. Our candidate pool is composed of those with an excellent ethical reputation and a solid track record of competence. We select the temporary leader from this pool based on the fit between the person's gifts and the challenge we face right now.
After a necessary struggle to exchange information about our immediate and larger situation, we graciously cede leadership to the next generation. The young

genuinely honor the old for the challenges they have overcome, since the young richly benefit from what their elders achieved.

The old genuinely honor the young for the challenges they must overcome, since they know generations of work can be lost if they fail.

Day 342

God's happiness travels to us along the path of the "we" signal coming into and out of our minds. It is two-way communication. God called us into service. We call out to God daily.

"God, please help us. We pray for grace and wisdom. Help us see, feel, hear, know, understand, respond, become, and embody what is true and useful to you and your purposes."

The greater the sense of "we," the larger the field of life we include in our own sense of well-being, the closer we are to God's heart.

The closer we are to God's heart, the stronger the happiness we will carry, in the form of wise kindness.

Day 343

The world thinks happiness follows the "me" signal.
They are half-way right. There is no "we" without
strong, functional individuals.
It is possible to have a "me" without a "we," though not
a healthy one. It is not possible to have a "we" without
a "me" combined with at least one other "me."

A chain really is only as strong as its weakest link. The
stronger the individual units and the working bond
between them, the stronger the local "we" unit, the
greater the challenges it can undertake.

The weakest link is always a "me" who does not trust or
seek God's ethical guidance.

We want strong, competent, confident individuals who
think independently, while staying dependent on God,
and upholding our standards of conduct.

Day 344

High diversity with low cooperation is chaos. Chaos pulls everything apart. It is a sign that chaos rules when aggression is celebrated over assertiveness. There is enough competition in nature for each creature to gain and hold its own, given space, but no more.

Only habits of cooperation are strong enough to deal with an environmental threat larger than any individual can cope with, no matter how aggressive the individual is.

Any newcomer is welcome whose differences bring new ways to cooperate and construct a larger, stronger happiness for all of us.

Any newcomer whose differences only bring new ways to be harmfully uncooperative will be confronted immediately. We will make it clear that such behavior will not be permitted when we meet to solve problems and make decisions. If the newcomer's behavior does not change they we ask them to take their chaos somewhere else where that behavior is normal.

Day 345

High cooperation with low diversity is stagnation. Stagnation celebrates passive acceptance of the way things are, no matter how wasteful or unjust. In nature standing water breeds nasty things.

Since the pie never gets bigger in a stagnant culture, "success" is getting a bigger piece of the shrinking pie through clever politics.
Corruption and self-dealing are everywhere in stagnant societies.

The mark of a stagnant society is permanent, multi-generational, unearned privilege alongside permanent, multi-generational, unearned misery.

As the cancer of stagnation grows, an ever-smaller group of people get way more than they need, at the expense of an ever-larger group who get less than they need.

We detect the beginnings of stagnation and stop it before it starts. Waste is what tips us off. When we see wasted lives, resources, and opportunities we speak up.

We huddle and work together to make the system better.

Day 346

In nature "affinity" is the name of the force that brings components together and keeps them together. Affinity brings creatures to cooperate and keeps them together in a state of productive cooperation.

Affinity comes from direct contact with a practical problem we all share, but none of us can solve on our own. It is not imaginary or contrived. It is not the need to perform rituals or ceremonies. The pull of affinity comes from a real problem, something that threatens our survival, growth and development if not solved.

Day 347

Affinity is an invisible force strong enough to pull us together, but not so strong that it crushes all individuality, initiative, and innovation. Rather than suppress original thought, affinity stimulates it. Affinity arrives in the form of a compelling question. Why is it that...? Why can't we...? How might we...?

Where there is affinity, there is no disagreement that the problem exists. A problem is the gap between what needs to be happening and what is happening. Where there is affinity there will be engagement rather than indifference. There will be productive disagreement over what is causing the problem and how best to solve it. Each of us brings a piece of the puzzle and needs the others to put together a working solution.

Affinity supports and fuels work. In working together, we test each other's ethics. If someone only has "me" ethics it will be miserable to work on anything together. If someone has both "me" and "we" ethics it will be fascinating to work on something together.

Working together is the only thing that builds real, durable trust, which allows real friendship to grow.

Real friendship is the only thing that dispels loneliness. There is no real happiness without friendship, so God never brings us together without putting us to work.

Day 348

Affinity is a gift from God. Oddly enough, it starts with fear. There is a real, legitimate fear of the consequences for all of us if we can't solve the problem facing us. We put the problem in front of us and face it side by side.

We don't waste time facing off against each other. We make the problem the problem, not each other or our differences in outlook. We look for clues to the solution in our differences because God has hidden them there.

Affinity alone achieves high diversity and high cooperation. It is one of God's masterpieces. As God rebuilds us through the process of redemption, we develop a natural affinity for each other and the work we are called to do together. Affinity feels like affection and a sense of belonging.

Even when we get stuck for long periods, we don't give up. We have a conditioned confidence that God is with us.

Day 349

Where we get stuck there is darkness, polluted air, coldness, and heaviness. Where we break through there is light, fresh air, warmth, and sudden lightness. We soar. There is laughter. There are tears of joy. It is the experience of salvation.

Salvation is a sudden expansiveness, a sudden opening from above. It is the feeling one has who has been buried under the rubble of an earthquake the moment they are found and pulled out. There is light, warmth, lightness, and clean, crisp air.
Salvation has nothing to do with an afterlife. Salvation happens in this life, for this life, in service of all life. You aren't saved so you can go shopping. You are saved so you can be helpful to life.

Where real salvation is happening the behavior of individuals and groups is a true credit to God, not an embarrassment that has to be denied and excused.

Day 350

Salvation is also the experience of a seed that has been dormant for years, looking dead.

Then suddenly, under the right conditions, the seed germinates. The hard, drab shell falls apart and drops away. Fresh, green, new life explodes out into the sunshine, growing exponentially in the blink of an eye.

Those of our kind who went before us have left seeds of insight buried in their notes.
We pick up where they left off and add our own insights to it. With this new combination, things happen we never could have imagined and in ways we never could have anticipated. The plan is clearly not ours but rather is held in the mind of One vastly superior to our own.

We feel the exhilaration of unforeseen, unplanned new life unfolding. We must rush to catch up!

Where real salvation is happening the activities of individuals and groups are new, relevant, and fascinating, not a mechanical show on display in a quiet museum.

Day 351

Salvation comes from following the clues in the "we" signal. Openings into God's happiness come after we heed the correcting, directing "we" signal, no matter what the cost. The "we" signal follows the path of least resistance through the most available soul and most available group. Resistance is anything that redirects our attention and makes us unavailable.

Saving breakthroughs do not happen among the stagnant and tradition bound, who live in books. There is too much arrogance and stubbornness. It is just too cold.

Saving breakthroughs do not happen among the chaotic, chasing their private dreams. There is too much selfishness and rivalry. It is just too hot.

Day 352

More than half of our bodies are made up of water in its liquid form. All of the processes of life depend upon water, but not in the form of ice or steam. Tradition is ice, manic chaos is stream. A higher, better combination of diverse lives is not possible in a stagnant or chaotic place.

New life needs enough stability to get going while it is small, weak, and vulnerable. It also requires the right temperature, not too hot and not too cold. Chaos won't provide enough stability and is too hot.

New life needs enough space to grow once it gets started. Stagnation won't provide enough space and is too cold.

God's presence among us keeps us warm enough to stay fluid. God's presence among us opens us to new spaces large enough to give our new growth a home.

Like liquid water, we have enough structure to move into new spaces and take on new forms, but not so much we can't change, or so little we can't get anything done because everyone does whatever they want without coordinating their actions.

Day 353

When we see a top athlete in action we see grace. We see power under precise purposeful control. One form of grace shows up at the start of an athlete's development and another form shows up at the peak of development.

Early grace is the innate kinesthetic intelligence she was born with combined with an environment that stimulated and developed her kinesthetic intelligence. She did nothing to earn it. It was given to her. She has no memory of not having access to it. She was too young to pay for it, it was provided and managed for her.

From there she enters a long and rigorous development process. She activates all her muscles groups until she can feel them firing in unison. Next she adds resistance training to build strength in each group. Next she learns to rally as much force as she can in as little time as possible. The most force possible in the least amount of time possible is called power.

Finally comes late grace. She practices using her power with great precision to astonishing effect.

We follow the same developmental process individually and as a colony. We begin by carefully observing and nourishing the unique gifts each one has, starting at home with our children, then extending out to any learning experience we provide for children.

We have learned that it is usually an unplanned event that activates an innate ability. In these surprising events we sense the active involvement of God.

Day 354

Something new happens that activates our inborn ability to seek and receive God's signal. It is usually a surprising setback of some kind.

We feel that pathway fire in our brains. Something new comes alive in us.

Next we must overcome internal and external resistance to thinking this new way, again and again, until seeking God is a stronger habit than ignoring God.

Next we must put this habit to the test when unforeseen setbacks occur. We must rally our learned confidence and face the crisis now with no time to prepare.

We find our love for God is powerful enough to get us through.

Finally, we are given an opening to use these new capacities to provide just the right service, at just the right time, fast enough, to make a difference that could have come about no other way.

We perform gracefully and then graciously direct any admiration that may come our way back to God, the original source of all that happened.

We have come full circle.

Day 355

In nature there is no grace that absolves a creature of the need to learn and grow. There is also no growth that requires no grace to get started. In nature there is only *graced growth*.

Solid growth comes through struggle to solve problems and overcome obstacles. But struggle alone cannot provide the essential ingredients we will use in the struggle. Those are given to us by another.

A gracious person is a grateful person. We are a grateful and graceful people. We know God gave us gifts and opportunities to cultivate them. We did not give those things to ourselves. We return the favor with graceful, elegant behavior that produces useful outcomes. We have come full circle.

We also recognize the gifts of others and repay our debt to God by creating opportunities for them to cultivate their gifts. We feel happy when they become more competent and confident, not envy.

We feel God's smile when we rejoice in the happiness that growth brings to others. It means we have become truly helpful.

Day 356

The work God entrusts to us is bigger than any one individual or group can do. It must be handed off to another whose job it is to correct it and take it farther. Consistent high quality is a function of thoughtful, careful handoffs from one person to another, one function to another, one group to another, one generation to another.

If my partner cannot do her work well and on time until and unless I do my work well and on time we have a *working handoff* to manage. We are interdependent. We refine our handoffs until they work reliably. If she has part of the answer and I have part of the answer, but we don't have a complete answer, we have a *learning handoff* to manage.

We refine the way we exchange information until we have the best working model possible, one that corresponds as closely as possible to our shared, changing reality.

Day 357

A handoff is a living agreement between two equal and autonomous parties. It must be constantly updated to make sure it meets the needs of both parties to ensure the success of their shared effort. Like a relay race, it can all be won or lost in the handoffs.

Handoffs must happen between groups that depend on each other's work. Handoffs must happen between succeeding generations of a people whose calling will take centuries to fulfill.

Handoffs are never left to chance in nature. Good handoffs are what make habitat safe and resource rich. Good handoffs are what makes home feel like *home*.

We seek God's guidance on how to make all our handoffs work to serve God's purposes, because it is in handoffs that the work is most at risk. But it is also in handoffs that we see God has made profound structural change.

Our highest loyalty is now to the well-being of whole, to our sense of "we." In the tension of handoffs, we see whether it is still all about "me."

Day 358

To feel *at* home does not mean I *am* my home. To be *at* peace with my partner does not mean I *am* my partner. We remain two different, separate entities, but we still enjoy contact with each other.

To be *at* home with God is not to *be* God, it is to be *with* God in a way that works for both you and God.

God's happiness comes from staying by God's side and on God's side in every contested issue. God always sides with all of life. So do we.
We stay by God side, ready to do whatever God wants done, God's way. In this way we are *at* one with God.

At-oneness with God is the only atonement there is and the only one that works.

Day 359

We have come a long way this year, but we have only just begun to know God. God conceals and God reveals. We must never overestimate our understanding of God or God's intentions. Undue familiarity and smug certainty about God's plans combine to form a closed system, a stagnant pool that breeds deadly pathogens.

We feel God's personality as we seek and receive direction. That does not mean God is reduced to a person, our personal buddy. At court we may feel the personality of the judge, but we would never enter acting like buddies with the judge. We never forget the vast difference between ourselves as creatures and God as Creator.

That feeling of personality is merely an access point God put in our brains so we could connect with any other mind, including God's. My house *has* a door, but my house is *not* a door.

God is infinite and eternal. We are finite and mortal. There is only so much we will ever know, but it is enough to fulfill our purpose as earthlings.

Day 360

In the presence of The Creator, we are dumbstruck. Words fail us. God exceeds the holding capacity of any language or art.

God is not a he, a she, a they, or an it, and will not be limited to any of those notions, although from time to time we may feel something that seems masculine, feminine, collective or like an invisible force.

God is in nature but is not the same as nature, because God is not created. The Creator is also beyond, before and after anything created.

Day 361

When we don't know for sure that things will turn out to our advantage, we are facing an ambiguous situation.

We are being restored to God's original design for our species when we can happily engage an ambiguous situation without doing any harm to life, any life. Instead, we instinctively seek God's ethical guidance. We wait to feel the "we" signal directing us to find new, uncopied, unforeseen ways to be helpful.

All creators start with unformed material. A sculpture starts with a block of stone, a painter with a blank canvass, a musician with a ready keyboard. The raw, unformed material of creation is any situation that is fluid, emerging and ambiguous.

If the situation is not harmful, just ambiguous, it is something entrusted to us by God. We have been given a job to do and a place and time to do it in. If we rise to meet the situation quickly, with little or no complaint, we have been fitted to join the work.

It is a privilege to assist the Creator in the work of creation, not a burden.

Day 362

Earth has had many ages, defined as a periods of marked change in the processes and events that affected the entire planet.

A look at where the word "world" comes from reveals a temporal idea, not a spatial one.

"World" originally meant "the age of man." The age of man to date is marked by a recurring pattern of growth, destruction, and collapse. Why is that?
All solutions humans use to create their "world" require constant inflows of energy, time, and attention to maintain. Once there are more solutions to maintain than there are resources to maintain them, the solutions start to fail, one by one, each pulling down the one that depends on it.

Then come the shocking blows delivered by nature, and the self-inflicted catastrophe of war.

If there was just one crisis to deal with, humans could rally their resources to meet it. It is not possible to deal with a large number at once, especially when there is no consensus on which ones are most important.

Day 363

It is observable, factual, and logical to acknowledge that we are approaching the end of the world, the end of the age of man. It is magical thinking to believe otherwise. There is no mystical, magical "we" that is going to show up through mobs, majorities, and markets to fix everything, restoring it to what it was.

No technology will do it for us. Technology is more likely to eliminate us than save us.

Yet the earth is not approaching its end. Life finds a way, it always has. The earth will survive and recover without this version of humanity, but the reverse cannot be said.

Earth has kept in reserve a previous version of humanity that is now being activated. They live hidden in obscurity, in vanishingly small numbers, spread over a vast area. They are called earthlings.

Day 364

Godless worldings are headed where the world is headed. Godly earthlings are headed where earth is headed. We will each share the ultimate fate of what we identify with, depend upon and feel most deeply attached to.

It is an act of God's mercy to be prevented from getting more involved with a worldly endeavor. It doesn't make you a loser, it prevents you from losing everything. You were saved and preserved to enjoy a different fate.

There is news to report. The court has issued its final ruling of the session. In a unanimous verdict nature, history and conscience all declare:

From this day forward, God's people are to be released from slavery to the world.
They are free to go out and participate in Earth's future, under certain conditions.

As a called, redeeming, and happy people, they have been placed all over the earth in small working colonies. Two of them aiding each other is partnership. Three of them aiding each other is a colony. Until they can consistently create and maintain justice among three souls, they are forbidden to add more people to the colony.

But once they can consistently maintain God's happiness between them, they are free to use what they have been given to participate in the greatest and final reversal primates will experience in their tenure on earth.

Day 365

We have our orders.

We cannot change or save the world. It is possible to keep a safe distance, but it is not possible to stop an avalanche once it starts.

But life still makes sense and tells us what we *can* do, what we were *made* to do. We can rejoin the earth on life's terms to help restore the earth. Only God knows the specifics because the events we will respond to creatively haven't happened yet. Where we are headed no tradition can guide us, only God can.

We have a learned confidence that there will be an opening, just big enough, lasting just long enough for the godly to pass through to a very different age. Afterall, we will be needed on the other side of this frightening passage.

There will be much hard work to do. That is what we were saved and set aside for.

Once we are reconnected to earth, working under God's direction, fulfilling the role designed for us, earth can enter an age in which its full creative potential can start to unfold.

We will function as catalysts, as earth's keystone species.

As godly earthlings, it will be our privilege to help usher in the Age of God.

Afterword

As a kid there was a moment when I *already* had the ability to ride a bike but hadn't yet felt it. I just knew riding a bike was possible because my friends were having fun riding their bikes. Knowing I was missing out was motivating and gave me the courage to risk failure and even injury. I wanted nothing more than to take part in the activity of bike riding.

To get started I needed someone who already knew how to ride a bike to hand that skill set off to me. I needed help, but only so much.

With some training wheels and my big brother running alongside, I learned how to use my body to operate the device. Then we removed the training wheels. After putting in effort, enduring some frustration and surviving some accidents, suddenly something from inside took over and I was riding my bike! On my own! I wasn't thinking about how to do it, my body just somehow knew what to do. I outran my brother and never looked back. I have no memory of what happened to the training wheels.

It was thrilling. It was liberating. A new larger world opened to me. I joined my friends in the neighborhood who had gone before me.

Over the past year I hope this book may have served a similar function. You may want to read this through again for several years, but once you experience God's happiness for yourself, once you feel it at work in you and around you, this book should become redundant. You will probably forget where you put it.

The way God does happiness moves from your brain to your body, from words to deeds, from deeds to habits, from habits to instincts.

Living this way will just *feel* right, and living any other way will just *feel* wrong. The farther you go, your own discoveries will take you further than this book can, and will be better anyway, because they will fit your specific unfolding situation, which I never could have anticipated.

I received help from countless people for decades. My wife and daughter helped me get out of God's way in our family and helped me convey each idea in this book. As best we could, we wanted you to have a clear line of sight to the glory of life lived on God's terms.

We feel a natural desire to participate in life, to imitate and extend the helpfulness we have experienced. We decided what we could do was try to help you find and awaken what is already inside you.

A new year awaits.

What can you make of it?

In Friendship,

Tim Daniel

A note from Abbey:

Getting started in a regular conversation with God can feel overwhelming. I didn't know how to fit it into my schedule or how to start. It is especially hard for folks like me who didn't grow up in church I didn't know how to pray. I asked Dad to help, and he provided me with a simple prayer to use daily. He suggested starting each day with this prayer at a set aside time when I could be rested and quiet.

"God I know I don't know what is best. I pray for grace and wisdom. Please help me today to see, hear, feel, know, become and enact what is useful to you and helpful to life."

This prayer has never gone unanswered.

dod yn ôl at fy ngho